Phyllis Vos Wezeman
Anna L. Liechty

HYMN STORIES for Children

Resources for Children's Worship

kregel
RESOURCES

Grand Rapids, MI 49501

Hymn Stories for Children: Resources for Children's Worship
by Phyllis Vos Wezeman and Anna L. Liechty.

Copyright © 1995 by Kregel Publications.

Published by Kregel Resources, an imprint of Kregel Publications, P.O. Box 2607, Grand Rapids, MI 49501. Kregel
Resources provides timely and relevant resources for Christian life and service. Your comments and suggestions are
valued.

Cover Photograph: © William Hebert 1994
Cover Design: Brian Fowler/THE DESIGN TEAM
Craft Illustrations: Judith Harris Chase
Book Design: Alan G. Hartman

Library of Congress Cataloging-in-Publication Data
Wezeman, Phyllis Vos.
   Hymn stories for children: resources for children's
worship / Phyllis Vos Wezeman; Anna L. Liechty.
      p.   cm.
   Includes bibliographical references.
   1. Worship (Religious education). 2. Hymns, English—
History and criticism. I. Liechty, Anna L. II. Title.
BV1522.W48   1995   264'.2'07—dc20   94-37816
                                          CIP

ISBN 0-8254-4022-x (paperback)

1 2 3 4 5 Printing / Year 99 98 97 96 95
Printed in the United States of America

Table of Contents

Introduction

There are many available resources that trace the stories behind the hymns that we sing in worship. However, most Christians do not know the stories, and certainly most children have not heard or read them. Since these hymns are the basis for much of the message of our faith and are an integral part of worship, they seem a logical place to derive ideas for the children's message or for a children's worship time.

The basic approach of *Hymn Stories for Children: Resources for Children's Worship* is to outline a children's message using an object lesson related to a familiar hymn text. A unique part of these children's messages is that directions for making the object are provided so the teaching tool also be used as a learning activity in church school classes, children's church, or family activities.

Included are directions for creating the object or teaching tool, a suggested script to be used with the children to convey the story of the hymn, and instructions for leaders so they can prepare for their presentation. To reinforce the message, each child may be given directions for creating his or her own story-related object either in church school, in children's worship, or at home with family. Of course, to connect the lesson with the words of each hymn most effectively, an effort should be made to sing the hymn in worship, in classes, or at home.

The following is a suggested script for introducing the concept of *Hymn Stories for Children:*

[Hold up a hymnal.] What is this? [Give the children time to answer.] Did you ever think about how a book like this gets started? Each of the hymns in this book is a story because each hymn was written by a person trying to tell the story of our faith. Over the years these hymns became a part of our church's story. Maybe you have a favorite hymn that you like to sing—and that way hymns become our stories of faith, too. What we are going to do together is to look at some of the most famous hymns we sing, maybe learn some new ones, and find out the story behind each hymn.

Hymn Stories for Children: Resources for Children's Worship invites all ages to hear the message of faith behind the words we often sing. More than just hearing, however, participants can become involved in creative experiences that celebrate both the people whose hymns we share and the God whose name we praise.

To Don and Linda LeMahieu

for sharing faith and friendship. (P. V. W.)

In loving memory of

my maternal grandfather, Ernest Ralph Biggs, who could sing hymns from one church on his circuit to another and never sing the same one twice. (A. L. L.)

Special thanks to

David S. Wezeman and Keri A. Wolford for research assistance. Educational Ministries, Inc. for permission to print material published in *Church Worship*.

All Creatures of Our God and King

Background Information

Composer: Francis of Assisi (1182–1226)
Year of Publication: 1225
Tune: From "Geistliche Kirchengesung" (1623)
Scripture Reference: Psalm 145:10–11

Theme

The beauty of nature inspires us to praise the Creator.

Teaching Tool

diorama

Suggestions for Dialogue and Discussion

Today we are going to learn the story behind the hymn "All Creatures of Our God and King," written nearly seven hundred years ago. Let's put the background on our diorama while we learn the background of the story. The man who wrote this hymn, St. Francis of Assisi, was the son of a wealthy family in Italy and grew up very spoiled and privileged. Then, Francis discovered the joy of giving to the poor and serving the Son of God. All of his life, St. Francis found God's presence in the beauty of nature around him, even calling the sun his "brother." [Hold up the sun (a purchased sticker, a cutout from yellow construction paper, or draw the sun as the story is told).] The first thing to put in our diorama is the sun to remind us that St. Francis was the *son* of a wealthy cloth merchant, a follower of the *Son* of God, and a man who saw the beauty of God's creation in the *sun*. In fact, another name for this hymn is "Canticles of the Sun," and it was written on a hot summer's day.

Like all creatures on earth, St. Francis did not always have sunny, easy days. Some times were dark and difficult. Of the sixty hymns he wrote, St. Francis wrote this hymn toward the end of his life when he was sick and nearly blind. Yet even then he found joy in the gifts of creation, like the moon and the stars that give light in the darkness. [Place the moon and stars on the "night" side of the diorama.]

As St. Francis traveled with his friends, he saw all of creation as symbols of love: God's love for us and our love for God. What favorite parts of creation represent God's love to you? Flowers? Trees? Grass? St. Francis saw these gifts of nature as our most precious possessions; he chose to live without money, to live simply and take care of the poor. It made St. Francis sad when the noblest creatures—humans—failed to praise God. [Add nature artifacts or cutouts to represent the joy of creation in the diorama. If desired, add the figure of St. Francis as well as the figure to represent the participant.]

As we sing "All Creatures of Our God and King," we should remember how important it is to praise the God of creation. In the beauty of this season, we should listen and observe St. Francis's words: "Let all things their Creator bless . . . Alleluia!"

Materials

- wooden clothespins with rounded tops
- pipe cleaners
- fabric scraps
- yarn
- scissors
- markers
- shoebox
- construction paper
- glue
- natural objects like leaves, pebbles, grass, flowers, pine cones

Method

Create a diorama as a setting for telling the story that celebrates the gifts of creation. In advance or during the storytelling, form the background by covering a shoe box with construction paper. Inside the box, cover half with light blue and half with dark blue or black to suggest day and night. To decorate the inside, draw, cut from paper, or purchase stickers that suggest the elements of nature honored in the song. Another option is to include real specimens of nature in the diorama. In addition, a small figure can be added to the scene representing St. Francis or the maker of the diorama or both. Draw a face on the rounded top of the clothespin. Twist a pipe cleaner around the neck to form arms. Cut a 2" x 6" rectangle of fabric. Fold it in half and cut a small slit in the center. Slide the head through the opening. Arrange the material over the arms. Secure it in place by tying a piece of yarn around the middle. Use yarn glued to the top of the clothespin for hair, gluing it in a circle for Francis to create a "bald spot."

Amazing Grace

Background Information

Composer:	John Newton (1725–1807)
Year of Publication:	1779
Tune:	"Amazing Grace"—an early American folk melody
Scripture References:	1 Chronicles 17:16–17; Ephesians 2:8

Theme

No one can boast before God; each one of us is saved only by the grace of God.

Teaching Tool

walnut shell boat

Suggestions for Dialogue and Discussion

Can you read the name on my little ship? [Hold up the walnut shell and wait for responses.] The name of a ship is often found on the prow. Of course this isn't a real ship—but it still has a name, the *John Newton*. That's because John Newton is the author of the words in the hymn we are going to sing today. He was also a sea captain of a much larger boat than this. John Newton had been at sea since he was eleven years old. He was a hard, unhappy person. The ships he sailed carried slaves to sell. That was a really bad thing to do, wasn't it? Once when John Newton was at sea, the most terrible storm he had ever seen made him fear for his life. He began to pray in earnest to be saved. When the storm was over, he was still alive, but he was a changed man.

You see, he discovered something called God's *grace*—the free gift of God's love and mercy that God gives even though we don't deserve it. That grace is amazing! And that is the title of the hymn that John Newton wrote. [Add the sail with the words *"Amazing Grace"* already written.]

John Newton was so changed by his experience of God's love that he stopped sailing slave ships. In fact, he stopped sailing altogether and went to school. It took him sixteen years because he had dropped out of school at age eleven, but he finally became a minister of the Gospel in the Anglican church in England. People came eagerly to hear the words of the former salty sea captain. He never tired of telling about God's amazing grace. He even wrote poems to use in his sermons, over three hundred of them, but "Amazing Grace" is the one that is still sung and remembered today.

John Newton lived to the ripe old age of eighty-two. Even when he became so old and had to be helped into the pulpit to speak, he never tired of reminding his listeners that he could at least remember two things: "I am a great sinner, and Christ is a great Savior! What amazing grace!"

On that stormy sea when he reached out to God, John Newton discovered a new direction for his life. It was as though he raised the sail of faith and the wind of God's Holy Spirit began to steer John's life on a new course. He not only turned his back on the slave trade, he also persuaded William Wilberforce to stay in politics, and he worked with him to abolish the slave trade. It is probably fitting that the tune used with "Amazing Grace" comes from the American south and the folk music of the plantations. Even more interesting, the year John Newton died—1807—was the year that England abolished slavery forever. When we let God's Spirit chart our course, there is only one word that describes the great things He can do with sinners like you and me, and that's—*amazing*!

Materials
- walnut shells
- modeling clay
- scissors
- construction paper
- markers
- toothpicks
- tape or glue

Method
On half of a hollowed out walnut shell write the words *John Newton*. Place modeling clay in the bottom of the walnut shell. Cut a sail from construction paper and write the words *"Amazing Grace"* on both sides of it. Glue or tape the sail to a toothpick. Push the end of the toothpick into the clay to hold the sail in place.

Be Still, My Soul

Background Information

Composer:	Katharina von Schlegel (b. 1697) translated by Jane Laurie Borthwick (1813–1897)
Year of Publication:	1752, 1855
Tune:	"Finlandia" by Jean Sibelius (1865–1957)
Scripture References:	Isaiah 30:15; Proverbs 3:4–5

Theme

Trust in God brings beauty and peace to life.

Teaching Tool

breath painting

Suggestions for Dialogue and Discussion

[Hold up sample breath painting.] Do you like my painting? Well, I like it because I'm the one who created the design. I like the way the colors all blend around each other. Can you guess how I made this design? I didn't use my hands at all. [See if the children can figure out the method.] What I did was to begin with only three dots of different colors. [Hold up three paper circles of the colors.] Then I used a straw to blow on the colors so they moved around the page, blending and creating this pattern. It is interesting to see how it turns out because you can't tell at the beginning what exactly will happen.

The hymn we are learning about today has something in common with my painting. Three people played important parts in the creation of this hymn, but they didn't know each other at all; in fact, they lived in different countries at different times in history. The words to the song were first written by a woman named Katharina von Schlegel. [Turn over circle with name.] What country do you suppose she might be from? [Older children might guess "Germany."] Yes, she was a German Lutheran whom we really know very little about except that she wrote many hymns of faith during her lifetime. But we don't sing the hymn in German. That's where the next person comes in.

Jane Borthwick lived in Scotland nearly one hundred years later. [Turn over circle with name.] She was a scholar who knew German well. She translated many of the hymns from Germany for English-speaking people to sing. But she didn't write music.

We needed one more person to make our hymn complete. This person was Finland's best known composer, Jean Sibelius. [Turn over circle with name.] One piece of stirring music he wrote is called "Finlandia," and that is the tune to which we sing Katharina's words using Jane's translation.

Just like these three dots of color combined to create my painting, the efforts of these three artists blended to create the beautiful hymn "Be Still, My Soul." But I don't believe that happened by accident any more than I believe this painting happened by accident. I think God's Spirit caused the three artists' work to come together to create the beauty of our hymn. And I believe that is the way God works in our lives, too.

As we use our breath today to create beautiful designs, we can remember that God is in control just like our hymn says. If we give our lives to God like drops of paint, then God will guide and direct us and bring something of beauty to share with the world. Just like God gave us this hymn.

Materials

- white paper
- drinking straws; cut in half
- scissors
- food coloring in plastic bottles; blue, red and yellow
- construction paper; blue, red and yellow
- pens or fine-tipped markers

Method

Using three different colors of food coloring, one representing each "artist" in the hymn story, create a breath painting. Put a drop of food coloring on a sheet of white paper. Hold a straw perpendicular to the paper, with the end of the straw almost touching the food coloring. Blow through the straw to move the "paint" and to create interesting designs on the paper. Continue the procedure with the remaining two colors. Print the words *"Be Still, My Soul"* on the completed painting.

In addition, cut circles from blue, red, and yellow construction paper and write the corresponding words on the shapes:

- Blue—*Katharina von Schlegel; Poet; Germany*
- Red—*Jane Laurie Borthwick; Translator; Scotland*
- Yellow—*Jean Sibelius; Composer; Finland.*

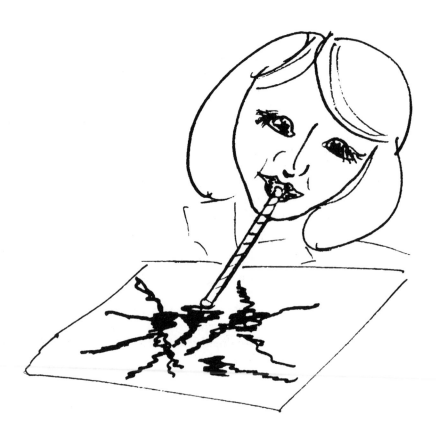

Blest Be the Tie That Binds

Background Information

Composer:	John Fawcett (1740–1817)
Year of Publication:	1782
Tune:	"Dennis" by Hans G. Naegeli (1773–1836)
Scripture References:	Romans 12:9–10a; John 13:34–35

Theme

Christian bonds of love bring strength and value to life, greater than anything the world offers.

Teaching Tool

friendship bracelet

Suggestions for Dialogue and Discussion

Do any of you have one of these? [Hold up sample friendship bracelet.] Does anyone know what this bracelet is for? [Someone may know it represents friendship.] Yes, a bracelet like this is called a "friendship bracelet" because it is usually made and given to someone as a symbol that your lives are connected by friendship. All of the knots represent the memories that bind us together as friends. That's a nice idea, isn't it? Christians are people who are bound to each other by friendship in Christ.

There is even a song that has been sung for over two hundred years about the special friendship that Christians enjoy, called "Blest Be the Tie That Binds." The man who wrote it, John Fawcett, was a Baptist minister in a small church in England. His family was growing and he was serving a small, poor congregation who couldn't afford to pay him enough to live on. Then he received a call from a large church in London. He was happy and began to plan to move. His congregation was saddened at the thought of their kind pastor leaving. They enjoyed his special gift for writing words for new hymns that they sang after the sermon each Sunday. But because they were loving folks who were bound together in Christ's love, they were willing to help their pastor move, even when they didn't want to see him go.

Finally the day came when wagons from the London church arrived to move John Fawcett and his family to their new parish. All the furniture and bundles were loaded on the wagon, except for one last box. John's wife looked thoughtfully at her husband and asked, "Are you sure we're doing the right thing? Where will we find a congregation with more love and help than this?" As they looked at the tearful faces of those they were about to leave, John knew the truth of his wife's words. The wagons were unloaded, and he and his family stayed among the people that had showered them with love. John Fawcett sent word to the London church that these were his "own people" that God had given him, and he needed to stay.

The next Sunday the sermon was entitled "Brotherly Love" which was also the title he gave to the new hymn the congregation sang that morning. Today we know that hymn as "Blest Be the Tie That Binds." Like the knots in our friendship bracelet, love's bonds hold Christians together in a support system that is more valuable than money or fame.

John Fawcett and his wife continued to minister to their small parish in Wainsgate, England, for more than fifty-four years. John became widely known as an excellent speaker, scholar, and writer. And even though King George III himself offered Fawcett any benefit he wanted, John chose to stay among the simple folk whose lives were bound to his by the strongest cord of all—love.

Materials
- embroidery floss; ten colors
- scissors
- cardboard
- tape

Method
Follow these directions to make a friendship bracelet.

1. Cut a 1 yard piece of embroidery floss from each of the ten colors.

2. Tie the ten strands of floss together and secure them to a surface such as a piece of cardboard.

3. Take the first strand, 1, and wrap it over, then under strand 2.

4. Hold firmly onto strand 2 while pulling up on strand 1 towards the large knot which was made in the beginning, step 2.

5. Repeat steps 3 and 4, making a second small knot on top of the previous knot. A double knot has been completed around 2. Drop strand 2.

6. Now take strand 1 and make a similar knot around strand 3, wrapping strand 1 over, then under 3. As before, make a second knot around strand 3 to complete a double knot.

7. Continue the rows in this way, making double knots with strand 1 around strands 4, 5, 6, 7, 8, 9, and 10. Strand 1 is at the far right side of the row when all double knots are completed.

8. With strand 2, work a second row of double knots, then with strand 3 work a third row of double knots, and so forth.

9. Continue until the tenth row is completed. One full color pattern has been completed.

Children of the Heavenly Father

Background Information

Composer: Caroline V. Sandell Berg (1832–1903)
Year of Publication: 1855
Tune: "Sandell"—anonymous Swedish melody
Scripture References: Matthew 18:14; Romans 8:38; 1 John 3:1

Theme

God's protection surrounds us like a loving father's reassuring strength.

Teaching Tool

paper circle cutout

Suggestions for Dialogue and Discussion

What shape is this card? [Most will recognize a rectangle.] This is a rectangle? Really? I thought it looked like a circle. Do you think I can make a circle from this card? [Most might say yes.] Do you think I can make a circle big enough to put your head through? [Most will say absolutely not.] Does that seem impossible? Well, I think I can do it.

But first, let me tell you about a woman who lived in Sweden many years ago. Her name was Caroline Sandell Berg. The hymn she wrote is called "Children of the Heavenly Father." It is a beautiful hymn about the protection and care God's love gives us. Her words remind us that nothing can separate us from God's care. Do you believe God can protect us, or does that seem impossible, too? [Fold and begin cutting the index card.] Caroline certainly believed God's promise, but not because God protected her from all the bad things that can happen in life. When she was a young woman, Caroline's father drowned. I am sure she was very sad. But Caroline didn't just give up on God or her faith. She discovered a great truth—that when we love God and we know God loves us, nothing can separate us from that love, not even death. Caroline went on to write over 1,650 hymns. She was even called "the Fannie Crosby of Sweden" because she wrote so many songs of faith for people to sing. That seems almost an impossible number of songs to write, doesn't it? But with God, all things are possible.

Do you still think it is impossible for me to cut a circle big enough to stick your head through from this small index card? [Finish last cuts, snip the inner folds, and carefully open the paper into a circle shape.] Look at this!

You see, it all depends on knowing how to make the right cuts. Just like in life, it all depends on knowing how much God loves us. Even when things seem impossible, if we trust God, just like a small child trusts his or her loving father, we will discover that God's love is encircling us, keeping us safe in the center of His will. [Place the circle over the nearest child's head.]

Materials

- index cards
- scissors

Method

Fold one index card in half lengthwise. Make the first cut from the folded side about 1/4 inch from the end. Cut straight toward the open edge, but do not cut all the way through! Leave about 1/4 inch uncut. Then, from the open side, cut back toward the fold, again allowing about 1/4 inch distance between cuts and from the edge. Alternate these cuts across the card. Be sure the last cut is done from the folded side. Leaving one loop intact at each end, snip through the rest of the loops down the center fold. Open gently to reveal a full circle.

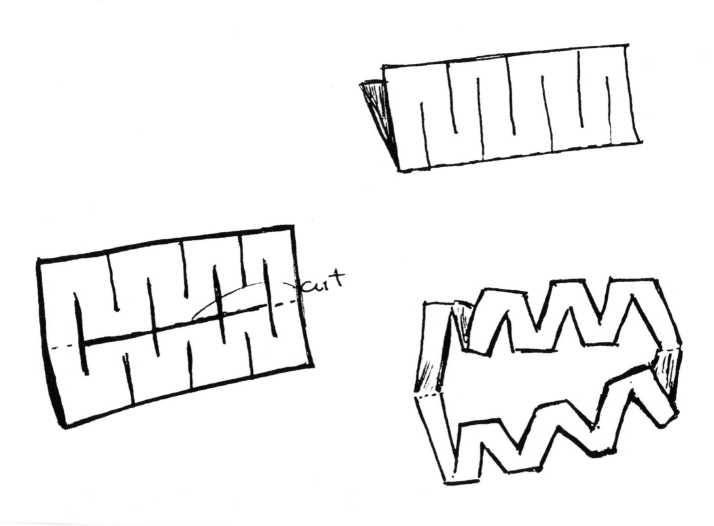

Christ for the World We Sing

Background Information

Composer: Samuel Wolcott (1813–1886)
Year of Publication: 1870
Tune: Italian hymn tune by Felice de Giardini
Scripture References: Matthew 28:19–20; Mark 13:10

Theme

Take the message of Christ to the world with zeal.

Teaching Tool

suitcase and folded bag

Suggestions for Dialogue and Discussion

How many of you like to travel? How do you feel when it is time to go someplace new and you pack your suitcase to go on a trip? [Pause for responses.] Do you feel excited? How about enthusiastic? I know a word that means excitement or intense enthusiasm. It begins with Z. Does anyone know it? It is *zeal*. When you have zeal you are intensely enthusiastic about something. And I want to tell you a story about someone who wrote a song about having zeal. His name is on this luggage tag. [Offer to let someone try to read it to the others.]

That's right. The Reverend Samuel Wolcott from South Windsor, Connecticut. At least that's where he was born. From the looks of this suitcase, he went lots of other places, too. He went to school at Yale and then to Andover Theological Seminary. [Point out these pennants or signs on the suitcase.] In fact, he became a Congregational minister and missionary. He went as far away as Syria. [Point to "Syria or bust" sign.] Why do you suppose he wanted to be a missionary? [Accept all suggestions.] I think it was because he had zeal. What did we say *zeal* means? [Intense enthusiasm] What do you suppose filled him with zeal, or enthusiasm? [Again, accept responses.] Well, Samuel Wolcott would probably tell you that his love for Christ filled him with an intense enthusiasm to share that love with people everywhere, especially those who had never heard about Jesus.

He had zeal to share the story of faith with the world. He probably took with him a suitcase. Now usually you put clothing in a suitcase, right? But this is a faith suitcase. And if you are going to share your faith with zeal, you must pack your suitcase with some special gifts of God. Let's open it and see what kinds of gifts Samuel Wolcott thought were needed to share our faith with zeal. [If time permits, let the listeners guess what ideas might be found there. Open the suitcase, pointing out that Z is for *zeal* and Z is for *zipper*. Take out the words written on construction paper one at a time and relate their meaning if necessary. Reward verbally those who guessed "love" or any other of the words.]

Samuel Wolcott went well prepared, didn't he? Due to poor health he didn't stay in Syria but came back to the United States where he was a minister in Providence, Rhode Island; Chicago, Illinois; and Cleveland, Ohio. [Point to those names on the suitcase.] In fact, in Cleveland he attended a Y.M.C.A. convention where he saw a banner displayed that said, "Christ for the World, the World for Christ." He was so touched by that message that he wrote a hymn called "Christ for the World We Sing" which immediately became a popular hymn about mission, or zeal, for sharing God's message of love and care.

You know, Samuel Wolcott was a missionary filled with zeal who lived a long time ago. But God needs people filled with zeal today, ready to take Christ's message with us wherever we go. God sent the Holy Spirit to fill us with intense enthusiasm or zeal for that very mission.

Now we can't really take a suitcase of love and joy and healing; those ideas have to be alive within us. But to help us remember to be open to the gifts of the Spirit and to be ready to carry intense enthusiasm with us, we can make a small bag and put in it reminders—anything that helps us remember to be filled with the zeal of God's Spirit.

Give each participant a square of paper and instructions for folding a bag. Folding the bag takes only a few moments. Then instruct everyone to place in the bag what fills them with zeal. They can print words and place them in the bag, or cut out pictures from magazines, or use pictures of Jesus or symbols from the church to fill their bags. Small pictures of earth would also be appropriate.

Materials
- Bible
- suitcase, preferably one that zips
- luggage tag
- pen
- adhesive-backed paper
- scissors
- construction paper
- marker
- tape
- 6" to 10" squares of paper for folding
- optional "fillings" for the folded bag: pictures from magazines, pictures of Jesus, Christian symbols

Method

Fill in the luggage tag with the following information: "Rev. Samuel Wolcott, 1813-1886; South Windsor, Connecticut." Place the luggage tag on the suitcase.

Make seven pennants from adhesive backed paper, or from construction paper that will be taped in place, that say:

Yale College; Andover Theological Seminary; Syria or bust; Providence, R.I.; Chicago; Cleveland; Y.M.C.A. Tape the pennants to the outside of the suitcase.

Write the following words on separate strips of paper and place inside the suitcase: *Love; Healing; Prayer; Redemption; Work; Joy; Song; Inspiration; Hope; Praise.*

Make an example of the paper folded bag. Using a square of paper 6 to 10 inches, fold and unfold the paper in half vertically and horizontally to find a mid point. Fold the top half in half again ("mountain" fold toward the back of the square). Fold in each of the top corners to the center crease. Fold in the bottom corners in like manner, only tuck the bottom corners underneath the flaps of the top fold. "Mountain" fold, then "valley" fold this diamond shape across the opening to create a flexible crease. Then open up the bag, ready to use. If desired, "Christ for the World, the World for Christ" can be written across the bag. If printed or colored wrapping or origami paper is used, start with colored side up.

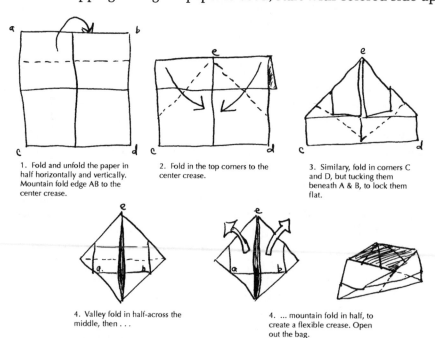

1. Fold and unfold the paper in half horizontally and vertically. Mountain fold edge AB to the center crease.

2. Fold in the top corners to the center crease.

3. Similarly, fold in corners C and D, but tucking them beneath A & B, to lock them flat.

4. Valley fold in half-across the middle, then . . .

4. . . . mountain fold in half, to create a flexible crease. Open out the bag.

Fairest Lord Jesus

Background Information

Text:	From *Munster Gesangbuch* (1677)
Year of Publication:	1677
Tune:	"Crusaders' Hymn"
Scripture References:	Colossians 1:16; Psalm 121

Theme

Faith in Jesus provides us with a source of strength and a shield for protection.

Teaching Tool

shield

Suggestions for Dialogue and Discussion

[Hold up a book of legends and folk tales.] How many of you like stories from books like these? [Discuss what legends are or let the children look for favorites. After the children have given responses, hold up a hymnal.] Our hymnal is another book of stories, and while the songs we sing are based on the truth of faith in God, some of what we know about these hymn stories is like our book of legends and folk tales. One of those legends concerns a hymn called "Fairest Lord Jesus."

This hymn was first written down in Germany in 1677, more than three hundred years ago. That's a long time ago, isn't it? But legend says that this hymn was first sung more than seven hundred years ago during something called the Crusades. Have you ever heard of the Crusades? [Allow the children to explain what they know or believe.] The Crusades were a time when Christians marched to the Holy Land—what we call Israel today—thinking they should fight to capture that land. Eventually, the people discovered that the Crusades were not a very good idea. During the 1200s, the legend says, a group of German Crusaders marched to Jerusalem while singing the hymn "Fairest Lord Jesus," so it is often called the "Crusaders' Hymn."

The Crusaders would probably have carried something that looked like this. [Hold up the cardboard shield. What is it? What is it for? Allow the children to answer.] The word *crusade* comes from a French word that means "cross." Do you see a cross on this shield? [Let the children point it out.] Most Crusaders would have had crosses on their shields, and then each area on the shields would contain symbols representing their faith and their families. [Either create each section of the shield while discussing the hymn, or if time is a constraint, present the shield already prepared.] This shield will remind us of the message of the "Crusaders' Hymn."

In this first section, we are reminded of who Jesus is. What symbols are here to remind us of Jesus our Savior? [Possibilities include famous representations of Jesus' face, a cross, a crown, a Chi-Rho, or other symbols for Jesus' name. Discuss the meaning of any symbols used.] The first stanza of "Fairest Lord Jesus" reminds us that Jesus is special to Christians; He is the focus for our worship and the source of our joy.

How much should we love Jesus? Well, the second stanza of the "Crusaders' Hymn" shows us how to love Jesus by thinking of the beauties of nature. What beauties of earth do we love? [Possibilities here are flowers, meadows, woods, streams, waterfalls, or other "pure" symbols of nature's goodness.] Taking a walk on a beautiful day can make us feel better when we're feeling sad, right? Jesus is even more beautiful and more pure than the best of nature; He can make our hearts sing.

What is greater than our earth? The heavens, right? If Jesus is fairer than our earth, is He fairer than the heavens, too? Our hymn says "Yes!" This third part of our shield represents all of creation beyond our earth. [Symbols here represent the universe as well as heaven itself, such as the sun, moon, stars, and angels.] Jesus is the Light of the World, and the third stanza of this hymn says that the light of Jesus is greater than all the lights of the universe—and even of heaven.

Some hymn books have a fourth verse of "Fairest Lord Jesus" that was added about two hundred years after this hymn was first written down. That fourth stanza is about offering our praise and adoration to God. So this fourth part of our shield represents us. Each of us must carry the shield of faith in Jesus into life's battles. But if we remember who our Leader is and how wonderful and fair He is, then we will go bravely forward with a song in our hearts, just like the Crusaders did so long ago. [Explain the symbols chosen to illustrate faith.]

Now our shield of faith is finished. As we sing "Fairest Lord Jesus" we can remember the legend about the Crusaders singing this hymn as they marched to Jerusalem. We can remember that Jesus is more beautiful to us than earth itself, or even the heavens, and that we are called to celebrate the gift of Jesus each day of our lives. Whether the legend of the "Crusaders' Hymn" is true or not, the message that it teaches us is true: faith in Jesus is the source of our strength and our joy. Faith is our shield—now and forevermore.

Materials

- cardboard or posterboard
- scissors
- markers
- construction paper
- symbol patterns or stencils
- old magazines
- glue

Method

Using the pattern provided, cut a shield from cardboard or posterboard. With construction paper strips or with markers, divide the shield into quadrants. The bisecting lines form the shape of a cross on the shield. Draw, trace, or cut out symbols that represent Jesus and apply them in the first quadrant of the shield. A cross and a crown are most appropriate. In the second quadrant, place pictures or symbols of creation, especially flowers and trees. In the third quadrant, place pictures or symbols of the heavens: sun and moon, stars, and angels. In the final quadrant, the maker should place pictures or symbols of himself or herself and family members.

Great Is Thy Faithfulness

Background Information

Composer: Thomas O. Chisholm (1866–1960)
Year of Publication: 1923
Tune: By William M. Runyan (1870–1957)
Scripture References: Lamentations 3:21–23; James 1:17, Isaiah 49:16

Theme

God's love sustains and renews us day by day.

Teaching Tool

paper plate story wheel

Suggestions for Dialogue and Discussion

What shape is the sun? [Hold up the story wheel with the opening at the yellow space. Students should say "a circle."] Where does a circle begin and end? [That should be a harder question to answer.] Circles don't really have a beginning or an end, do they? That could be the reason that a circle is a symbol for God. God is the same yesterday, today, and forever. There is no beginning or ending with God. That is why the circle behind the story wheel I have can remind us that God never changes.

Yet, for human beings there are changes. Each day is a new beginning. Is God's presence with us every new day? [Answers should be "yes!"] Of course! That is the message in the hymn "Great Is Thy Faithfulness." [Turn the story wheel to the section that names the hymn.] These words were written by Thomas Obediah Chisolm. And Thomas knew that he spoke the truth. Even though he was born in poverty in Kentucky and never had formal schooling after the eighth grade, Thomas became a teacher, newspaper editor, and a minister who wrote more than twelve hundred poems during his lifetime. He knew that God had helped him "morning by morning" every day of his life—and he lived to be ninety-four years old despite many battles with ill health!

When Thomas Chisholm had penned the words to "Great Is Thy Faithfulness," he sent them to a well-known man who published gospel music, William M. Runyan. [Turn the story wheel to Runyan's name.] Mr. Runyan was impressed with the simple message of the poem and prayed that God would help him write a worthy tune. The answer to his prayer is the music we sing today.

Although the sun casts a shadow as it turns, there is no shadow from the light God gives. We can see our blessings clearly if we think about God's gifts each new day, whether that day is in summer or winter or springtime or harvest time. [Turn the wheel appropriately for each season.] God also gives us the blessings of night, the moon and the stars. [Turn the wheel to the night sky.] In fact, everything in nature is a witness to God's love. [Turn the wheel to the nature scene.]

As well, we who turn to God each day are given a special relationship with God that means we can find strength to face whatever happens that day. [Turn the wheel to the cross.]

And now we are back to the beginning, just like a new day. When we think about all that God means to us and when we remember to be grateful for the joys and blessings that surround us every day, then we can begin to understand the deep faith of Thomas Chisolm that helped him praise God every day for ninety-four years!

Materials
- paper plates
- markers
- scissors
- magazine pictures
- stickers of nature pictures
- glue
- metal fasteners

Method

Construct a sample story wheel to use in telling the account of the hymn "Great Is Thy Faithfulness." Divide one paper plate into eleven equal sections. Beginning at the top of the plate and moving clockwise around the circle, write or draw the following words or pictures in each section:

1. Color the section yellow;
2. Write: *"Great Is Thy Faithfulness"*;
3. Write: *Thomas Obediah Chisholm;*
4. Write: *William M. Runyan;*
5. Create a summer scene;
6. Create a winter scene;
7. Create a spring scene;
8. Create a fall Scene;
9. Create a night sky;
10. Create a nature scene;
11. Draw or attach a cross.

Create the scenes by coloring the illustration with markers or by gluing pictures or attaching stickers in the appropriate sections.

On a second paper plate, cut away a portion the same size as one of the sections on the first plate. Position this plate on top of the "story scene" plate. Poke a hole in the center of the two pieces. Insert a metal fastener through the hole. Move the first plate, or wheel, to reveal the appropriate segment of the story as the account of the hymn is told.

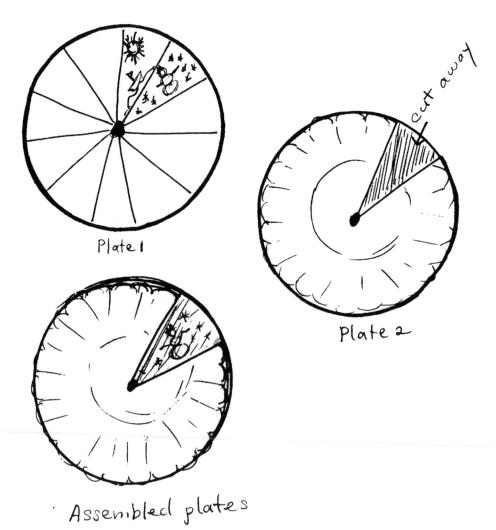

Plate 1

Plate 2

cut away

Assembled plates

Guide Me, O Thou Great Jehovah

Background Information

Composer:	William Williams (1717–1791)
Year of Publication:	1745
Tune:	"Cwm Rhondda" by John Hughes (1873–1932)
Scripture References:	Psalm 31:3; 1 Corinthians 10:1–4

Theme

Those who seek God's direction for life will be surrounded by signs of God's presence and power.

Teaching Tool

puppet mini-theater

Suggestions for Dialogue and Discussion

Here is a scene from the Bible about a very famous person who was guided by God. [Hold up sample mini-theater with the wilderness story depicted.] Can you tell what these pictures are supposed to be? [Listeners can name the cloud, fiery pillar, and rock.] Does anyone have a guess about who this person might be? [Let some take guesses; they may get the right name or they may suggest Jesus or other Old or New Testament heroes.] Those are all famous people that you mentioned and God certainly guided them, too, but this person is the one who led the children of Israel out of Egypt. His name was . . . [Tell them if they don't know.] Moses! Now Moses didn't have a compass or a map to help him find his way. In the heat and intense sunshine of the desert, all of the land starts to look alike. But God helped Moses and the people that Moses led. God shielded them from the heat with a cloud [move "Moses" under the cloud] and gave them a pillar of fire to follow, so they would always know which way to go. [Move Moses along the opening toward the fiery pillar.]

What is a big problem you can have in the desert? [There are many, but thirst or need for water should come up.] Right! When there was no water anywhere to be seen, God even helped Moses find a place to get a drink for himself and all the children of Israel. Can you guess where the water is in this picture? The water is hidden in the rock! Twice when they were desperate for water, God told Moses how to get water from a rock. It's interesting that we call Christ our Rock and also believe Jesus is our Living Water. There are many parts to the story of Moses and the Israelites being guided by God in the wilderness. They walked right through a sea on dry ground and were fed by food that fell from heaven called *manna*. Moses and the people of Israel were really guided by God, weren't they?

[Reverse puppet.] The story of Moses is a powerful reminder that God takes care of us even when the going is difficult. That is the message that a man from Wales learned when he was young. His name was William Williams. His father wanted him to be a medical doctor, and it was very difficult for him not to follow family tradition. God had called him to be a minister, however, and follow a different and difficult path. In addition to preaching, William used his gift of a beautiful singing voice to help other people find faith. He wrote over eight hundred hymns in his native Welsh, but "Guide Me, O Thou Great Jehovah" is his most famous. William knew that life is like a desert sometimes. He also knew the story of Moses in the wilderness and how Jehovah—or God—was with the Israelites. But William also knew that God still cares for people and leads them safely to find shelter [move puppet under the cloud], to find direction [make puppet follow fiery pillar], and God gives us the Bread of Heaven and the Living Water that we call Jesus to sustain us all our journey through. [Move puppet across the "stage."] So the "sweet singer of Wales," William Williams, wrote this hymn to remind the people of his day of the power and certainty of God's loving guidance. That's a message we need to hear today, too. When you make your own mini puppet theater, you can put yourself in the story, too. [Insert puppet with picture of storyteller.]

Materials

- drawing paper
- pencils
- markers or crayons
- tape
- scissors
- cardboard or cardstock
- tongue depressors or craft sticks
- glue

Method

Create simple rod puppets and a mini-theater to use while telling the story of the hymn "Guide Me, O Thou Great Jehovah." On an 8 1/2" x 11" sheet of paper, make large and colorful drawings of a desert. Include a cloud, fiery pillar, and rock. When the drawing is finished, use the ruler and pencil to draw a line across the bottom of the paper approximately 2" up from the bottom and 1" in from each side. Turn the drawing over and put tape across the area where the line was marked. Additional tape above and below the line will help reinforce the paper. Carefully cut along the strengthened line to form a slot at the bottom of the drawing. Set the illustration aside.

Form the simple rod puppets by drawing a picture of Moses on one side of a piece of cardboard or cardstock. On the reverse side, draw a picture of a man representing William Williams. Be sure to keep the figure size similar to those in the drawing. Cut out the shape and tape it to a stick. Use care to slide the puppet into the slot. Act out the story by moving the puppet back and forth through the scene. If desired, make an additional puppet representing the storyteller and insert it in the scene at the end of the story.

Have Thine Own Way, Lord

Background Information

Composer: Adelaide A. Pollard (1862–1934)
Year of Publication: 1907
Tune: "Adelaide" by George C. Stebbins (1846–1945)
Scripture References: Isaiah 64:8; Jeremiah 18:3–4

Theme

Because God chooses what is best for our lives, the Christian yields to God's molding like a potter who shapes the perfect vessel for his use.

Teaching Tool

modeling clay

Suggestions for Dialogue and Discussion

Do you like to work with clay? [Distribute a small portion of clay to each participant.] Do you know that scientists learn about people who lived thousands of years ago by studying the clay pots that can still be found buried in the earth? Clay has been an important creative tool for human beings almost since human beings began. [Encourage the listeners to begin to roll the clay in their hands to make it soft and shape it into a ball.] What happens as you work the clay? It begins to get softer and easier to work with, doesn't it? That is a pleasant feeling.

I want to tell you a story about a woman who was changed by God, like this clay is being changed in our hands. Her name was Adelaide Pollard. Well, actually, her name was Sarah, but when she grew up, she decided she liked Adelaide better than Sarah so she changed her name. During a time when women often didn't expect to have careers, Sarah—or, rather, Adelaide—took lessons in public speaking, moved from Iowa to the big city of Chicago, taught school, and even became a traveling speaker. She was a very determined woman! She worked very hard to raise money to travel as a missionary to Africa. I imagine she expected to make that happen, since she had accomplished all the other things she set out to do. That's why she became unhappy when those plans just didn't seem to work out. She must have felt crushed. [Flatten the ball of clay in the palms of your hands and encourage others to do the same.]

Sometimes our hopes get flat as a pancake, don't they? That is what happened to Adelaide. Then, one night at a prayer meeting, she overheard an old woman praying, "Lord, just have your way with our lives." Her words made Adelaide think. Later when she was reading her Bible, Adelaide came across the verses that compare God to a *potter*—a person who works with clay. She recognized that she had been trying to direct her own life and decided instead to let God mold and shape her. As a result she wrote the words to the song "Have Thine Own Way, Lord." Now that you have the clay flattened like this, you can begin to shape it into something useful—like a bowl or cup or pitcher. [Begin to round up the "pancake" shape to make a bowl. Permit potters to shape their own designs.] Now this shape, if we baked it or let it dry, could become a very useful container, right? [Display a completed clay container.] Well, that is what Adelaide found to be true in her life after she yielded her life to God. She did finally get to go to Africa. She also ministered in Scotland and later returned to travel throughout New England, sharing the message she had learned about yielding our lives to God's hands. She even wrote a number of hymns. But the one song she is remembered for, the most important message she left behind, is the song about recognizing that we are the clay in the hands of the Potter, "Have Thine Own Way, Lord."

Now that you have tried being a potter, you can remember that your lives are like the clay, and God can mold, shape, and direct your lives if, like Adelaide Pollard, you put yourself in God's hands.

Materials

- modeling clay
- completed clay container

Method

As the hymn story is told, shape a piece of modeling clay into a ball, then a flat "pancake," and finally a useful container such as a bowl or a cup. Complete a clay container to show during the discussion, too.

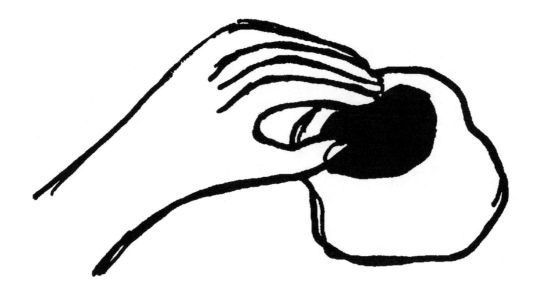

I Heard the Voice of Jesus Say

Background Information

Composer:	Horatius Bonar (1808–1889)
Year of Publication:	1846
Tune:	Originally "Vox Dilecti" by John B. Dykes (1823–1876)
Scripture References:	Matthew 11:28–29; John 4:14; 8:12

Theme

Jesus invites all to come to him to find rest, refreshment, and light for life.

Teaching Tool

a stole

Suggestions for Dialogue and Discussion

[Hold up a picture of a yoke of oxen or similar example.] Does anyone know what is in this picture? [Wait for responses.] Yes, this is a yoke of oxen. The wooden frame you see is called a *yoke* and is used to help the oxen work together as a team. It looks heavy, doesn't it? Do you think you would like to wear something like that? [Most will probably say "No!"]

Well, Jesus was a carpenter, so He knew all about making yokes for farmers to use with their animals. I'm told that if the carpenter fitted the yoke and balanced it just right, that the harness was not difficult for the animals to wear. Do you know that Jesus invites us to wear a yoke with Him? He says His yoke is "easy"—that it will fit just right. Life's burdens would certainly be easier if we let Jesus help us bear them, wouldn't they? In some churches the pastor wears a robe with a long, narrow cloth called a "stole" around the neck and over each shoulder. It is a reminder that Christians are called to be yoked to Jesus. We can also use this symbol from the yoke to help us remember Jesus' invitation and a famous hymn that was written by Horatius Bonar called "I Heard the Voice of Jesus Say." [Put on sample stole.]

Horatius Bonar was a Scottish minister who wrote words for over six hundred hymns. He wrote with children in mind because he was always concerned that young people like you learn about Jesus and the truth of Christ's life and work. So "I Heard the Voice of Jesus Say" is about the invitation that Jesus makes to Christians: "Come unto Me."

The first verse of the hymn is about hearing Jesus calling us to find rest. Sometimes in the journey of life we get tired and worn out. As we sing this hymn, we can remember that Jesus is calling us to come to Him. [Point to the top figure.] When we respond, we find a place to rest and lie down from our burdens, like a desert traveler who finds an oasis. [Point to the oasis symbol.]

The second verse of the hymn is about hearing Jesus calling us to drink living water. Have you ever been really, really thirsty? When you are very thirsty, a drink of cold water tastes so good. Our souls get thirsty, too. We sometimes go through a "dry spell" in our lives when we feel like we are "wilting"—we are just not getting what we need to live. Jesus says that He is the "Living Water" that refreshes us and gives us new hope. [Point to the water symbol.] When we say "yes" to Jesus' invitation, we find a cool drink of water that helps us to feel revived and ready to go on. [Point to cup symbol.]

The third verse of the hymn is about hearing Jesus calling us to Himself because He is light we need to see how to live. Sometimes we feel like we are in the dark and can't see which way to go to find our way through life's problems. Jesus says that He is the Light [point to the sun symbol] that can guide us and help us to see which path to take. [Point to the bottom figure.]

So each verse of "I Heard the Voice of Jesus Say" is about an invitation from Jesus to come to find rest, to find refreshing water, to find light for life. Like any invitation, Jesus' call, "Come unto Me," requires a response. If you listen to the words written by Horatius Bonar, you will discover the wonderful rewards of answering "Yes!" and of becoming yoked to Jesus. His yoke fits just right—He tailor-makes it for each one of us!

Materials
- felt
- scissors
- glue
- markers
- stole pattern
- symbol patterns
- picture of yoke worn by oxen

Method

A symbol stole will help the participants see and share a variety of themes related to the hymn "I Heard the Voice of Jesus Say." Using the pattern provided, cut a simple stole out of felt. As an alternative, the stole may be made out of pellon interfacing or paper. With the patterns as a guide, cut the six symbols from felt scraps. Add details and decorations to the pieces with markers. Glue the symbols to the two sides of the stole as illustrated on the diagram. Symbols on the right side represent Jesus' invitation. Symbols on the left side indicate the Christian's response.

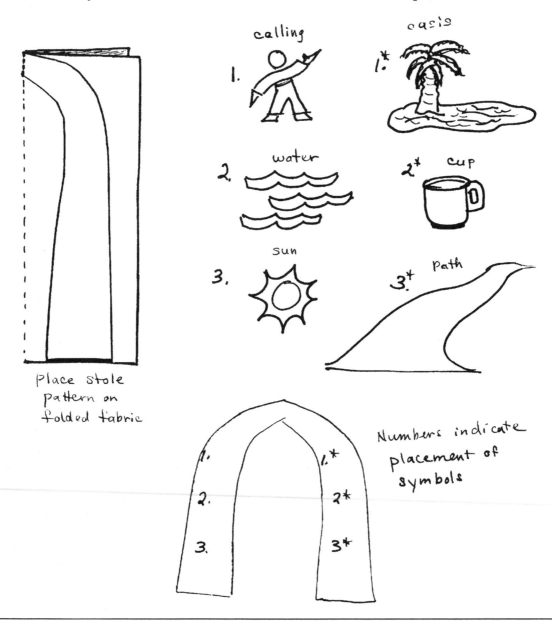

Place stole pattern on folded fabric

calling

oasis

water

cup

sun

path

Numbers indicate placement of symbols

I Love Thy Kingdom, Lord

Background Information

Composer:	Timothy Dwight (1752–1817)
Year of Publication:	1801
Tune:	"St. Thomas" by Aaron Williams (1731–1776)
Scripture References:	Psalm 137:5–6; Hebrews 10:24–25

Theme

The kingdom of God exists within us, around us, and beyond us.

Teaching Tool

castle

Suggestions for Dialogue and Discussion

I've added a few things to this box. Does it remind you of something? [Someone should say "a castle."] Right! This is supposed to look like a castle. Do you see any castles in your neighborhoods? Probably not. Castles were built a long time ago, weren't they? Who lived in a castle? A king or queen? Yes, the leader of a group of people like a king or queen would live in a castle. In the church we sometimes use the idea of a king and his kingdom as a way to understand God and where God lives. Of course, that doesn't mean God is a man—it's just a way to help us imagine an idea that is too big for us to understand. Coming to understand the kingdom of God is a lifetime occupation for the Christian.

The oldest hymn from American history in continuous use is called "I Love Thy Kingdom, Lord." [Point to hymn title.] It was written by Timothy Dwight, grandson of Jonathan Edwards who was a famous preacher from the earliest history of America. [Point to name.] Timothy would have made his grandfather proud because he was himself a Congregational minister, a legislator, and a teacher who eventually became president of Yale College. With the birth of the United States, the American church needed songs to sing that didn't remind them of England. So Timothy rewrote one of Isaac Watts' hymns about the kingdom of God, based on Psalm 137. [Point to words.] That helps us understand where the hymn comes from, but how do we understand the kingdom of God?

Each verse of the hymn reveals an idea about God's kingdom. First of all, the church is the people— you and me—the ones saved by Jesus. We are the "house" of God's abode, or dwelling. We must first accept God's authority in our lives. [Point to *personal*.] The kingdom of God is within us—our personal relationship with God.

The second verse speaks of the walls of God's church—the place where we come to worship. An important part of God's kingdom is each local congregation, the buildings where people gather to help and encourage one another as they seek God's guidance. [Point to *local*.] Just like this building we are gathered in today.

But God's kingdom is more than just a church building. The kingdom of God is all believers around the world, the church universal. [Point to *universal*.] God is the authority over all who believe.

So God's kingdom comes to earth through the faith of each person, each church, and all believers. Yet, God's kingdom is still more than we can imagine. God's power is eternal, so God's kingdom extends to heaven—the eternal dwelling for all those who are under God's authority. [Point to *eternal*.]

These verses in this old American hymn help us begin to understand the term *kingdom of God*. The church is nearly two thousand years old, even older than castles. And the church will continue because God lives within us, our congregations, and our world, for eternity. Our King is powerful beyond all understanding, and we are part of a kingdom that will know no end. No wonder the hymn is called "I Love Thy Kingdom, Lord!"

Materials

- cardboard box, 12" square (or larger)
- paper tubes, 2 per castle
- paper cups, 1 per castle
- toothpicks
- construction paper
- scissors
- tape
- glue
- markers

Method

Construct a simple castle from a cardboard box. Place a paper cup upside down on the top of the box to simulate a tower. Attach paper tubes as turrets on each side of the front. Cut two 4" circles; then make a 2" slit in each. Wrap each circle and glue or tape to create a cone shape. Affix to the top of the "turrets." Cut three small pennants from construction paper and write the appropriate words to share on each: *"I Love Thy Kingdom, Lord"; Timothy Dwight; Psalm 137:5–6.* Glue pennants to toothpicks. Add the toothpick flag with the hymn name to the paper cup. Attach the composer's name to one turret and the Scripture reference to the other. Glue in place. On the front of the box write *Personal*. Moving to the right, add one word to each side: *Local, Universal,* and *Eternal.* Add doors, windows, a drawbridge, or other details to make the box look more like a castle.

I Love to Tell the Story

Background Information

Composer:	Arabella Catherine Hankey (1834–1911)
Year of Publication:	1869
Tune:	"Hankey" by William G. Fischer (1835–1912)
Scripture References:	1 Peter 3:15; 1 John 4:9–10

Theme

Those who know Jesus find joy by sharing His story.

Teaching Tool

flip book

Suggestions for Dialogue and Discussion

Have you ever written a book? [Some may say "yes, at school." Invite discussion as time permits.] It is fun to tell a story for others to read and enjoy, isn't it? Books come in all kinds of shapes and sizes, about all sorts of topics. This is a book I made to help us learn the story behind today's hymn. [Hold up sample flip book.] Guess what the name of our hymn is? [Readers will be able to answer "I Love to Tell the Story."] I wonder who the person is who loves to tell the story? [Flip left side of book.] There is her name: Arabella Catherine Hankey. She had a nickname, though. Could you guess what it is? [Invite guesses; then invite someone to flip right side of book.] Her nickname was Kate. Kate was a born into a wealthy banker's family in England. She could have been anything or done anything that she wanted. [Flip left side of book.] What do you suppose was her mission in life? [Allow for guesses; then flip right side of book.] Kate's desire was to tell the story of Jesus to anyone who would listen. She must have been a very special woman.

[Flip left side of book.] Even good people get sick sometimes. Once Kate was very ill and spent a long time recovering. What do you suppose she did with her time? [After guesses, flip right side of the book.] She wrote two poems, one called "The Story Wanted" and the other, "The Story Told." These became her two famous hymns "Tell Me the Old, Old Story" and "I Love to Tell the Story."

But Kate not only loved to tell the story of Jesus [flip the left side of the book], she also lived the story. [Flip the right side.] Arabella Catherine Hankey lived out the Christian message as a Sunday school teacher among the poor in London, as a nurse in Africa and later in England, and as a writer, giving all of her income to missions.

Maybe we need to remember that all of us are writing a book—the story of our lives. And the choices we make about how we use our time, our energy, and our money tell others what is important to us. Kate's hymn and the story of her life should remind us of how a Christian's life story should be written—as a living tribute to the love of Jesus.

Materials

- cardstock
- duplicating equipment
- scissors
- hole punch
- metal rings, two per book

Method

Make and use a flip book to tell the story of the hymn "I Love to Tell the Story." Duplicate or copy the lists provided and cut apart the cards. Arrange the cards in the following order:

Left Side	Right Side
I Love to Tell	*The Story*
Arabella Catherine Hankey, also known as	*Kate*
Mission in life	*Telling the story of Jesus*
Once she was seriously ill	*Wrote two poems*
	that became her famous hymns
Lived the story	
	Teaching, Writing, Nursing, Giving

Leave two cards whole for the front and back covers. Punch holes in the cards as indicated on the illustrations. Attach the cut cards to the covers by inserting metal rings through the holes.

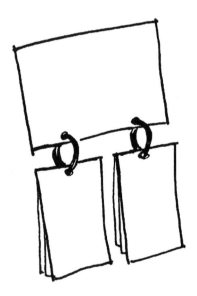

Jesus Loves Me

Background Information

Composer: Anna Warner (1820–1915)
Year of Publication: 1860
Tune: By William B. Bradbury (1816–1868)
Scripture References: Mark 10:16; 1 John 4:19

Theme

Each Christian is loved by God, who made each one unique.

Teaching Tool

thumbprint heart

Suggestions for Dialogue and Discussion

[Hold up heart shape.] I bet everyone recognizes this symbol. What is it? [Allow someone to answer "Heart."] And the heart shape symbolizes what? [Someone should say "Love."] Yes, this symbol means "love." If you were going to think of someone who loves you, you might think of your parents or grandparents, or sisters or brothers—but in the church we know who it is who brings us God's love best. Who is that? [Children should know that it is Jesus.] Yes, Jesus loves us. We know that, don't we? Jesus came as a human being to show us God's love.

There is something special about being a human being, something that distinguishes each one of us. And that is a fingerprint. So to remind ourselves that Jesus was a person who came to earth to show us God's love, let's make a fingerprint stamp right here in the middle of this heart, okay? [Choose a child or make the first thumbprint yourself.]

Isn't that neat? Do you know that each and every person has a different fingerprint? No one else's fingerprint is exactly like yours. God made each one of us unique. And Jesus loves each one of us, just as we are. Let's stamp a second fingerprint right above the first one to remind us that each of us is loved by Jesus. [Choose a child or make the second thumbprint yourself.]

That really is the heart of the Christian message—Jesus loves me. Is there a song you can think of that tells that story? That's right! There is a song called "Jesus Loves Me." The song was first a poem in a story written by Anna Warner together with her sister Susan Warner. They both became famous authors in the middle 1800s. "Jesus Loves Me" was a poem spoken to a sick child in their book *Say and Seal.* The sisters had been left penniless when their parents died, but they were people of strong faith. They taught Sunday school classes to young cadets at West Point and used their unique gifts of writing to share the message of Jesus' love. They were both loved by their students and were even given full military honors at their funerals. To remember Anna and Susan Warner, let's put two more thumbprints on our heart, one on each side of our first two stamps. [Add two thumbprints to the design.] Is this starting to remind you of something? It looks like a cross, doesn't it?

If you think it looks like a cross, you are right. We just need to add one more stamp to our heart. This stamp completes our design, and it reminds us that the poem "Jesus Loves Me" became complete when a man named William Bradbury set the words to music and added the chorus "Yes, Jesus loves me. The Bible tells me so." With his contribution, the song "Jesus Loves Me" became an immediate success. It has since become one of the most famous hymns sung all around the world. It is often the first song sung by missionaries to new Christians. A professor very knowledgeable about the Bible always reminded his students that the greatest truth in the Christian faith could be summed up in the words: "Jesus loves me; this I know."

Now you know the story of this famous hymn. And you can see another symbol inside our symbol for love: the symbol of the cross, our reminder of just how much Jesus loves us—each one of us is "thumbbody" special to Him!

Materials

- construction paper
- scissors
- stamp pad
- wet paper towels
- markers

Method

Fold a piece of construction paper in half. Draw a heart on one side of the paper, making sure that the left side of the shape touches the fold of the sheet. Cut out the symbol. Using a washable ink stamp pad, place the thumb on the pad and then make a print in the center of the front of the heart. Form a cross shape by adding thumbprints around the four sides of the center impression.

Write information about the hymn "Jesus Loves Me" on the inside or the outside of the paper. The completed project may be used as a greeting card.

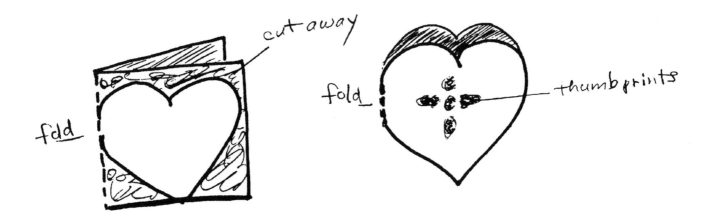

Jesus, Priceless Treasure

Background Information

Composer:	Johann Franck (1618–1677)
Year of Publication:	1653
Tune:	"Jesu, Meine Freude"—German melody arranged by J. S. Bach (1685–1750)
Scripture References:	Matthew 6:19; Luke 12:34

Theme

Peace comes to those who discover the eternal treasure of Jesus' love.

Teaching Tool

song lyrics

Suggestions for Dialogue and Discussion

Have you ever followed a pattern for anything you've made? [Prompt suggestions if necessary, like for stenciling, sewing, cutting, or tracing.] Why is it good to follow a pattern? [Listeners should suggest the idea that a pattern helps you make things more accurately.] It is hard to explain exactly how a pattern works, isn't it? But we often need a pattern, especially when we try something we've never done before.

A long time ago a man in Germany liked to write hymns for people to sing. Johann Franck wrote one hundred hymns to express his faith, but he is remembered primarily for one special hymn he wrote called "Jesus, Priceless Treasure." For that hymn he followed a pattern. He took a love song that people liked to sing and turned it into a love song about Jesus. [Hold up posterboard with Johann Franck's words.] That was really smart, wasn't it? Songs that people already know help them sing and remember a new message. Johann Franck wanted to remind people that the love of Jesus was more valuable than any other because Jesus' love will never fail us. Treasures like peace, security, forgiveness, love, and true friendship can only come from God. And those are treasures that cannot be taken from us. Do you think that is an important message to help people remember? I think so. Do you suppose we could follow a pattern like Johann Franck to help people remember the priceless treasure of Jesus' love?

I started a song to the familiar tune of "Jesus Loves Me." That's a melody we all recognize, right? Certainly we need to sing about how much Jesus loves us, but maybe we should also sing about how much we love Jesus. How about if we sang words like this [hold up posterboard with words and sing together]:

> Jesus is my truest friend
> His love for me will never end.
> Each day I offer Him my love.
> He gives me gifts from God above.
> Jesus my treasure!
> He's all my pleasure.
> Jesus my treasure!
> I love Him more each day.

Maybe you would like to write your own words to this tune or to another one. The important idea is that we can use patterns to help tell others about Jesus, like Johann Franck did with the hymn "Jesus, Priceless Treasure." And we can follow the pattern of Jesus to become a more loving, caring Christian, sharing the gifts of love and forgiveness that are God's gifts to us in Christ. That would certainly make the world a richer place, wouldn't it?!

Materials

- music to selected song(s)
- posterboard
- writing paper
- markers
- pens

Method

On a sheet of posterboard, copy the title and words to the first verse of "Jesus, Priceless Treasure." Place the name of the tune, *"St. Thomas,"* in the right hand corner, and place the name *Johann Franck (1618–1677)* in the left hand corner. Copy the new words sung to "Jesus Loves Me" on another sheet (or on the back) of the posterboard. Provide posterboard or paper for individuals or groups to write additional verses.

Jesus Shall Reign

Background Information

Composer:	Isaac Watts (1674–1748)
Year of Publication:	1719
Tune:	"Duke Street" by John Hatton (c. 1710–1793)
Scripture References:	Psalm 72; Philippians 2:10–11

Theme

Christians are appointed to share the news that Christ is King of all the earth.

Teaching Tool

kite

Suggestions for Dialogue and Discussion

Kites have been around for a long time. Did you know that? Missionaries—people who take the story of Jesus all around the world—even used kites to help people understand about God. They would get the people they were trying to teach together to fly a kite. They would let each one have a turn holding the string to feel the tug of the kite dancing high in the air. Then, they would let go of the string. What would happen? The kite would keep soaring higher and higher until no one could see it anymore. Then the missionaries would say, "Do you believe the kite still exists even though you can't see it?" And the people would answer, "Yes!" Then they would be ready to understand that they could believe in Jesus even though they couldn't see Him.

On Pentecost Sunday in 1862, the people on one of the South Sea islands sang an opening hymn at the very first worship service after their king and leaders became Christians. Over five thousand people sang the words that Isaac Watts had borrowed from Psalm 72: "Jesus shall reign where'er the sun does his successive journeys run."

In our day and age when we are used to satellite dishes that transmit information instantly around the world, it is hard for us to imagine what it was like when most people in the world had never even heard of Jesus. Isaac Watts took the words from Psalm 72 that were a prophecy about the coming Messiah or King and used them to tell the news that Jesus is the King of all the earth. This hymn is called the first missionary hymn. You see, in Isaac Watts' day there were no missionaries. No one was taking the message of Jesus' love to faraway places. It was fifty years after "Jesus Shall Reign" was written before the first modern missionaries began to visit other lands with their message of faith and their lesson of the kite.

Flying a kite is an excellent way to understand the meaning behind today's hymn, first because a kite soars high above the earth where many people can see it from great distances. If all Christians would let their faith in God soar like a kite, then the message of God's love could be seen around the world. Also, the kite represents the message we have to share because hidden inside it is a cross. [Turn kite over to reveal wooden cross.] The reason that Jesus shall reign is because He has triumphed even over death. And finally, kites soar because the wind holds them up. As Christians, we know that the wind of the Spirit lifts us and fills us with the energy we need to share the message that Jesus is Lord. Isaac Watts used the words from the Psalms that were thousands of years old to proclaim the importance of missionary work that really didn't even begin until after his death. Who knows to what great heights God will lift us? Because God is King of all the earth, God can do anything!

Materials

- sticks or dowels, two per kite
- newsprint, wrapping, or tissue paper
- cloth scraps or crepe paper strips
- nylon cord or heavy string
- markers
- scissors or knife
- stapler and staples
- glue
- ball of kite string

Method

To make the kite frame, cut small slits in the ends of two sticks. Securely lash together the sticks, forming a wooden cross in the process. Stretch a long string taut through the slits to form the frame. Lay the frame down on paper and draw around it, leaving an extra inch on all sides. Cut a V-shape out of each corner so the paper will fit around the sticks better. Decorate the paper before attaching it to the frame. Write *"Jesus Shall Reign"* in the center of the kite. Add additional information about the hymn around the border. *N, S, E, W,* for North, South, East, and West, may be written on each point. Attach the paper to cover the frame. Carefully fold down edges and glue or staple them to the sticks. Reinforce the edges with tape. Tie a few cloth or crepe paper strips together for a tail and attach it to the kite. Cut a length of string for the bridle and tie one end to the top of the spine and the other end to the bottom. Before flying the kite, tie a ball of kite string to the bridle.

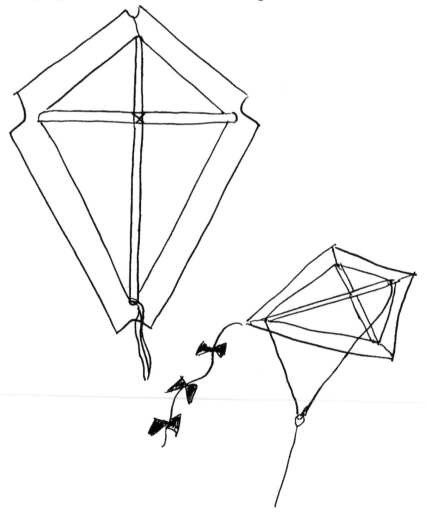

Joyful, Joyful, We Adore Thee

Background Information

Composer: Henry van Dyke (1852–1933)

Year of Publication: 1911

Tune: "Hymn to Joy" melody from Ninth Symphony by Ludwig van Beethoven (1770–1827)

Scripture References: Psalm 98:4; Luke 19:37–40

Theme

Creation's response to God is joyful praise.

Teaching Tool

rhythm instrument—shaker

Suggestions for Dialogue and Discussion

I'm going to count to three, and then I want all of us to take a deep breath, okay? One . . . two . . . three . . . breathe! Do you know what we just demonstrated? We all were *inspired* at the same time! Have you ever been inspired before? Well, of course, you breathe all the time. But to be inspired is to draw a breath in joyful surprise. [Illustrate.] Ahh! Do you know when I am inspired? When I see a beautiful sunrise or sunset, or when I sit by the lake and listen to the breeze in the pine trees. [Or use suitable personal examples.] Most people might say they are inspired by beautiful scenes in nature. Something happens inside us when we are inspired that is difficult to explain. But we recognize the joy! Maybe we feel joy because we recognize the presence of the Creator in special moments like those.

That is what happened to a man named Henry van Dyke. He was a well-known Presbyterian minister and an English professor at Princeton University. He had written many devotionals and even a short story called "The Other Wise Man." But he is most remembered today for the words to a hymn he was inspired to write by the beauty of the Berkshire Mountains of Massachusetts. When he handed the words of his new poem to the president of Williams College where he was the visiting minister, he said "This must be sung to Beethoven's 'Hymn to Joy.'" His visit to those mountains inspired one of the church's most loved hymns, "Joyful, Joyful, We Adore Thee." You see, when Henry van Dyke admired creation, he recognized in the beauty and joy of nature the hand of the Creator. [Hold up the sample shaker and point to the pictures.] In the same way, when we see the beauty of nature around us, we can be inspired to praise our Creator God.

When we are inspired, we want to respond in some way. That is a natural longing. In fact, Jesus said when His disciples were excited and joyful in His presence that if they didn't shout their praises, even the very rocks would cry out in praise of God! That seems impossible to us, but God sometimes allows the impossible to happen. The very music that we sing in "Joyful, Joyful We Adore Thee" should have been impossible to create. You see, Ludwig von Beethoven was completely deaf when he wrote his Ninth—and final—Symphony. Even though he could not hear the music with his ears, Beethoven could still feel the inspiration of the poem, "Ode to Joy," that his friend Friedrich Schiller had written. His response to that inspiration became some of the greatest music ever written.

We can respond to God's inspiration, too. Sometimes we want to make a joyful noise to let others know how excited we are. The Bible says that is one way we can respond to God—with a joyful noise. Let's finish our rhythm instrument by adding some small stones—reminders that all of creation responds to God, like the Berkshire Mountains or the stones that Jesus talked about. [Allow children to begin adding stones.] Years ago, a person who could not hear at all was said to be "stone deaf." The stones can also remind us that Beethoven was "stone deaf" when he created the beautiful music that we sing today. [Secure the top in place and shake.] And now we can make a joyful noise as we celebrate and praise our God!

Materials

- potato chip or juice can with removable plastic lid
- construction paper or adhesive-backed paper
- scissors
- glue
- nature pictures or stickers
- stones or pebbles
- permanent markers

Method

Create a rhythm instrument shaker to illustrate the hymn story "Joyful, Joyful We Adore Thee." Begin by covering a potato chip or juice can with construction paper or adhesive-backed paper. Decorate the can with magazine pictures or stickers of nature scenes, especially mountains. Using permanent marker, write information about the hymn, such as the title and the composers, on the lid of the can. Fill the can with small stones or pebbles. Secure the cover in place.

My Faith Looks Up to Thee

Background Information

Composer:	Ray Palmer (1808–1887)
Year of Publication:	1832
Tune:	"Olivet" by Lowell Mason (1792–1872)
Scripture References:	Romans 5:1; Hebrews 11:1

Theme

When we hold on to faith, we are sustained by God.

Teaching Tool

pocket heart

Suggestions for Dialogue and Discussion

What do you carry in your pockets? Does anyone carry a pocketful of faith? [Pause for responses, most might say "no."] How would you carry a pocketful of faith? That seems pretty difficult, doesn't it? Maybe even impossible? I know a story about a man named Ray Palmer who once carried his faith in his pocket. [Point to his name on the pocket heart sample.]

Ray Palmer was a young man who had just graduated from college. It hadn't been easy for him to get his education because his family had many financial problems. But Ray had wanted to be a minister. He felt God had called him to preach the gospel. But in order to survive he had taken a job teaching school. It was very difficult for him. He became ill and very discouraged. What do you do when you feel hopeless? Do you write poetry? That's what Ray Palmer did.

Ray wrote about what he had that was keeping him going. What do you suppose that might be? [Point to the word *faith* on the pocket heart.] Right! He quickly wrote down lines that came to him about all the times he knew faith was the key to finding help—times like when we sin and feel separated from God, when we lose the energy to live what we believe, when we face problems and feel lost, or—finally—when we face death. In all of those times, we must have faith to survive. But faith in what—or whom? [Point to *God* on the pocket heart.]

Right! Our faith must be in God. On our pocket heart the word *God* is above the word *faith*. The name of the poem that Ray Palmer wrote was "My Faith Looks Up to Thee." We must look up to God to find strength for life. Ray knew that. But he needed to write it out to remind himself. So he put the words to his poem in a little notebook; he carried it in his pocket every day for two years. Then guess what happened.

A friend of his named Lowell Mason [point to his name on the pocket heart], who was a well-known hymn writer, asked Ray if he had any poems that might make good verses for hymns. Hesitantly—because he never really meant to share what he'd written—Ray took his poem from his pocket and showed it to Lowell Mason. Mr. Mason was so impressed he copied it down right then and there and went home to write the tune we call "Olivet" as special music for such inspiring words.

Ray Palmer discovered something that is a good lesson for all of us. Our faith in God is important and should be with us everyday. But if we share that faith with others, then we supply others with a blessing that may reach far into the future. Although Ray Palmer did become a Congregational minister and wrote other poems, hymns, and Christian essays, he touched the most lives by the simple sharing of words of faith from his own need for God—found right in his own pocket.

You can make a pocket heart, too, and fill it with your own poem of faith or with a copy of Ray Palmer's words. I'm sure he wouldn't mind!

Materials

- felt, fabric interfacing, or construction paper
- scissors
- glue or stapler
- trims such as lace, rick-rack, or buttons
- markers
- paper
- pens

Method

Make a pocket heart by cutting fabric or paper into 6" x 12" or 12" x 18" pieces. Fold the material in half vertically and cut the top to a rounded shape. Unfold. Bring the bottom of the material up to the top and crease. Next, fold the lower right and left corners toward the center and crease. Fold the top flap of the material down and glue or staple it in place. Write the word *God* on the top of the heart, *Ray Palmer* on the left side, *Lowell Mason* on the right side, and *Faith* on the flap. Decorate the heart with a variety of trims. Carefully open the pocket. If desired, write a poem about *faith* or copy stanzas to the song "My Faith Looks Up to Thee" on another sheet of paper. Fold up the sheet and place it in the heart pocket.

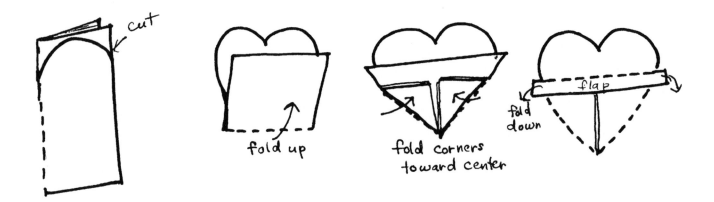

Nearer, My God, to Thee

Background Information

Composer:	Sarah F. Adams (1805–1848)
Year of Publication:	1841
Tune:	"Bethany" by Lowell Mason (1792–1872)
Scripture References:	Genesis 28:10–22; John 1:50–51

Theme

God reveals the path to those who seek His Presence.

Teaching Tool

ladder

Suggestions for Dialogue and Discussion

Have you ever climbed a ladder? [Hold up sample of "Jacob's Ladder."] Would the first step be at the top or at the bottom? [Likely, the response would be "at the bottom."] Well, it would depend if you were coming down or going up, wouldn't it? But most of the time, we would consider the first step to be the bottom rung of the ladder. We use ladders for lots of things. Did you know there was a famous story in the Bible about a ladder? Yes, it's the story of "Jacob's Ladder." [Point to the words written on the sides of the ladder.]

Jacob had a dream. You see, he had done a wrong thing and was running away from God. When it got dark, he lay down on the ground with a stone for a pillow. That sounds pretty uncomfortable! But while he slept, he dreamed of heaven opening and a ladder coming down to the spot where he slept. He even saw angels coming up and down the ladder. That's a pretty remarkable dream, isn't it? Jacob was so impressed that God would offer mercy to him even when he didn't deserve it that he made a promise right then and there to choose to accept God's offer of love. And he placed a marker in that spot and called it *Bethel*, which means "house of God."

Many sermons have probably been preached about Jacob's ladder, but one time a minister asked a friend if she knew of any good hymns about the story that he could use to conclude a worship service centered around Jacob and his experience at Bethel. Although his friend, Sarah Flowers Adams, told him she didn't know of any such hymns, his question so inspired her that she sat right down and wrote the words to the hymn "Nearer, My God, to Thee." Who do you suppose provided her with that inspiration? Do you think it was from God? I do. You see, like in Jacob's dream, the help comes down to us from heaven. That's why these words are written from the top of the ladder down. [Point to the words on the rungs of the ladder.] It is God who opens the way and offers us the ladder. But like Jacob responded to God's offer, Sarah had to take the first step and sit down to write the words that came to her. That's the way God's ladder works—the way is offered, but we must choose to take the steps to follow and be nearer to God.

Have you ever felt like Jacob—knowing that you've done something wrong, something sinful? God will forgive you even when you feel like you don't deserve it, just like He forgave Jacob. He has opened the way through His Son, the Lord Jesus Christ.

Jesus once told a man named Nathanael, "You shall see heaven open, and the angels of God ascending and descending on the Son of Man" (John 1:51 NIV). Jesus was saying that He was like that ladder in Jacob's dream. Through Him we have the way to God. He gives us His love and forgiveness, but we must choose to come to Him.

Materials

- craft sticks or tongue depressors
- markers
- glue

Method

Form a ladder from craft sticks or tongue depressors to use as the illustration for the hymn story "Nearer, My God, to Thee." Write the following words on separate sticks:

- *Jacob's Ladder*
- *Genesis 28:10–22*
- *God (reverse side—Jesus)*
- *Jacob (reverse side—Nathanael)*
- *Bethel (reverse side—John 1:51)*
- *Sarah Flowers Adams (reverse side—Us)*

Glue the pieces together to form a ladder, using *Jacob's Ladder* and *Genesis 28:10–22* as the sides, and the other four sticks as the rungs. Be sure to place *God* at the top!

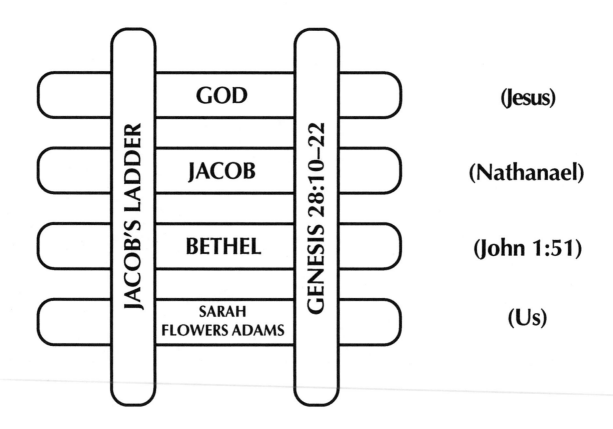

O Jesus, I Have Promised

Background Information

Composer:	John Ernest Bode (1816–1874)
Year of Publication:	1868
Tune:	"Angel's Story" by Arthur Henry Mann (1850–1929)
Scripture References:	Luke 9:57; John 12:26

Theme

In response to Jesus' love, we promise to follow and to serve, but we can only keep that promise with the help of Jesus.

Teaching Tool

sealed note

Suggestions for Dialogue and Discussion

Have you ever gotten a note that had a seal on the back like this? [Hold up sealed note.] Most likely not. But in days gone by, before envelopes with glue on them, people sealed notes with wax and their own special designs so that the person who was to read the message knew no one else had broken the seal and read the contents. The special design of the stamp, the tool also used to mark the sealing wax, let the receiver of the note be sure of the identity of the person who had sent it. The stamp and seal was sort of a promise that the message was real and to be believed. We still "seal" and "stamp" our letters today—but in different ways. This note is stamped with a cross; shall we break the seal and see what the note says? It seems to be addressed to us. [Open seal.]

The note reads: "Dear Friends, Follow Me," and it is signed "Jesus." And here's another note inside. This one is already open. It is dated 1868 and signed by an Anglican minister named John Ernest Bode. It's written to his three children, a daughter and two sons, who were all to be confirmed on the same day. It reads, "Dear Children, I have written a hymn containing all the important truths I want you to remember when you are fully confirmed."

Well, I have to admit I made these notes, but the words in them are real. Jesus really does ask those who believe to follow Him. And a man named John Ernest Bode really did write a hymn named "O Jesus, I Have Promised" for his three children on their confirmation day. His church and many churches today have a special service for young people who have chosen to follow Jesus. They are *confirming*—sealing—the promises made for them by their parents when they were baptized as infants. Many other churches have a special service for babies called a *dedication service* where the parents promise to provide a Christian home and teach their children about Jesus. Later on we must each individually accept Christ and make our life-long commitment to Him. Whatever our church tradition, our parents can help us know about Jesus, but we must each choose to trust and follow Him.

Here is another note. This one is addressed to Jesus, but right now it is blank. You see, each of us must respond to Jesus' invitation to follow. What John Bode taught his children in the hymn is that believers can say "yes" to Jesus because Jesus Himself will stay near to help us keep the promise.

So we have three notes, representing three parts to a very important promise. The first part of the promise comes from God who makes us His own and promises to be our God. The second part of the promise comes from those who bring us to God, most often our parents, that they will raise us to know God and teach us the way of faith. The final promise—the one John Bode's hymn is about—is our response to God's love. Each one of us must make the promise for himself or herself. We promise that we will follow and serve Jesus wherever He leads—but we have the assurance that Jesus goes with us to be our guide, our shield, and our friend. That seems like a pretty good arrangement—one worth setting our seal to.

Let's make our promise. [Write "Jesus, I promise to serve Thee to the end."] And mark it with our seal. The message is real and we mark it as our own. [Complete the sealing of the envelope as a group or individual project as is appropriate.]

Materials

- stationery or paper; three sheets per project
- pen
- envelope
- sealing wax or candles
- matches
- spools
- metal or wooden crosses
- glue
- foil
- newspaper

Method

Prepare a sealed note to use as the sample illustration for the hymn "O Jesus, I Have Promised." Fold three sheets of paper or stationery into thirds. On one piece, leave the inside blank, but write *Jesus* in the center of the outside. Fold up the sheet. On the second paper, write *Dear Children, I have written a hymn containing all the important truths I want you to remember when you are fully confirmed.* Place the date *1868* in the upper right hand corner. Fold this letter around the first note. On the third message, write *Dear Friends, Follow Me.* on the inside, and address it to the *Believers at [Name of Congregation]*. Fold the third letter around the other two notes.

Seal the parcel with the stamp of a cross. Construct the stamp by gluing a three dimensional metal, wooden, or plastic cross shape to one end of a spool. The spool serves as the handle for the stamp. Use commercial sealing wax or candle drippings for the project. If candle drippings are used, the wax must be very hot. Cover the work surface with newspaper. Light the candle, and carefully drip wax onto a piece of foil. Dip the stamp into the hot wax and immediately press the cross shape onto the letter, sealing the open edges together.

O Worship the King

Background Information

Composer:	Robert Grant (1779–1838)
Year of Publication:	1833
Tune:	"Lyons" arranged by William Gardiner (1770–1853). Attributed to J. Michael Haydn (1737–1806)
Scripture References:	Psalm 47:6–7; 104

Theme

No matter the height of human accomplishment, God's power and majesty inspire us to humble adoration.

Teaching Tool

cinquain poetry

Suggestions for Dialogue and Discussion

What is a word we can use to describe someone who has everything—wealth, fame, power, importance? [There may be little or no response.] It is very hard to find one word that says all of those things, isn't it? One way we have to express our feelings in the fewest possible words is called *poetry*. In the Bible, the Psalms are poems that seek words to say what God is like. It would be even harder, wouldn't it, to try to find one word to express what we feel about God?

There was once a man who was born into a family of wealth and honor and who became very important. You probably have never heard of him. His name was Robert Grant. He was born in India, but he was British. He was educated in England, became an attorney, and served in Parliament. He even was knighted, so he became Sir Robert Grant. He went back to India as governor of Bombay and became so well loved that when he died the people named a medical college after him. There are a few more things you should know about this famous man: he was also a poet and a devout Christian.

One time when Robert Grant was reading the Psalms—those poems in the Bible—he happened to read Psalm 104, that is written in praise of God. Robert was so inspired by those words that he wrote a poem to condense the most important ideas about God into just a few lines. The result was a hymn that we still sing today called "O Worship the King." *King* is a good word to use to try to say something about God—not that God is a man, but that God is all powerful, like a king. Do you suppose we could condense even the words of Robert Grant's poem to a shorter statement about God? Have you ever used a poem pattern called a *cinquain*? This poetry pattern challenges us to say everything we feel in just five lines using eleven words that follow a specific pattern. [Display the cinquain poetry pattern.] Just to show you, here is an example of a cinquain taken from "O Worship the King" [show the sample cinquain poem]:

God

Shield, Defender

Creating, Redeeming, Sustaining

The Ancient of Days

Friend

That pattern helps us focus on what we know and believe about God, doesn't it? Those feelings help us to worship—offer praise—to God. While you may never have heard about Robert Grant, even though he was rich and famous in his day, his poetry still lives on because he captured in words the feelings Christians share about praising God. You can write your feelings about God, too. Like Sir Robert Grant, you can use a Psalm that inspires you. Or you can choose just one word about God to say in a cinquain what you believe. Offering our words to God is one of the best ways we have to worship. And worshipping God is what is really important in our lives.

Materials
- posterboard
- markers
- cinquain poetry pattern

Method
Write a cinquain poem to help tell the story of the hymn "O Worship the King." Cinquain poetry follows this pattern:

Line One: One word title
Line Two: Two words that describe the title
Line Three: Three —*ing* words
Line Four: Four descriptive words that express a feeling about the title
Line Five: One word summary; synonym of the title

Copy the cinquain pattern onto posterboard. Also copy the sample cinquain poem onto posterboard to use while telling the hymn story.

God
Shield, Defender
Creating, Redeeming, Sustaining
The Ancient of Days
Friend

Open My Eyes, That I May See

Background Information

Composer: Clara H. Scott (1841–1897)
Year of Publication: 1882
Tune: "Open My Eyes" by Clara H. Scott
Scripture Reference: Psalm 119:18

Theme

To discover God's will for our lives, we must awaken our senses, waiting for the Spirit's touch with our whole beings.

Teaching Tool

body tracing

Suggestions for Dialogue and Discussion

Who do you know is a really good teacher? [Encourage responses.] Can you tell me why these people are good teachers? [Most of the reasons will be because the person is "fun, loving, or nice."] I am glad to hear you have good teachers because that is very important. One thing I know about good teachers is that they usually involve their students in learning with more than just one sense. They don't just make you listen or make you read. You will listen some, and read some, and also use your other senses like the sense of touch, smell, and even taste. People who know about how the brain works say that we remember better when more of our senses are involved in what we learn. Do you know who most people agree was the greatest teacher who ever lived? [Someone might guess "Jesus."] That's right. Jesus was a good teacher because He helped people to hear and see God's presence, but He also touched people's hearts as well, involving the whole person in experiencing God's love.

The song we are singing today was also written by a teacher, Clara H. Scott. She was a teacher of music at a women's seminary in the mid-1800s. She wrote lots of music, but the one hymn she is most famous for is called "Open My Eyes, That I May See." This hymn is really a prayer asking God to *illuminate*—bring light into—our lives so that we can know what God wants to teach us. Even the "teacher of the year" can't teach you anything if your senses are all closed off. And God doesn't force us to learn. So this hymn's message is an important one for Christians. [Hold up the folded body shape.]

This figure represents Christians like you and me when we are "closed off" from God. It is like we are all folded in upon ourselves, unable to learn what good thing God wants to show us. The song first asks God to open our eyes [lift head], our sense of sight. If we have eyes to see—not just looking, but really seeing—we will see God's presence in the world around us and in the people given us to love. Do you see God around you? If not, then maybe you need to sing this prayer for God to open your eyes.

We can also open our ears. When we begin to listen for God, then we can begin to respond to God's call in our lives. God calls us to follow. [Unfold legs.] Our ears opened to God allow us to be useful in God's world. God will call us to service.

Mrs. Scott's hymn also teaches us we must open our hearts to God's presence. [Unfold arms to reveal "heart" on the body.] Our feelings are not really in our hearts; that's just where the blood is pumped. But we use the heart that pumps our life-giving blood as a symbol for all of our deepest feelings—our very lives. The prayer of this hymn is that God will illuminate our very lives so that everything we do and say will be in response to the love God teaches.

Now our Christian is completely open. This is the way we best can learn of God—with all our senses, even our whole beings. Perhaps you would like to help each other make body tracings and then you can teach someone else how to open up to the message of God's love.

Materials
- butcher paper
- markers
- scissors

Method

Make a body tracing to serve as the illustration for the hymn story "Open My Eyes, That I May See." Precut a large body figure out of butcher paper or lie on the paper and have another person trace the shape; then cut out the figure.

Write the name of the hymn and its composer, Clara H. Scott, on the paper. Fold the arms in, the legs up, and the head down. These will be unfolded during the storytelling.

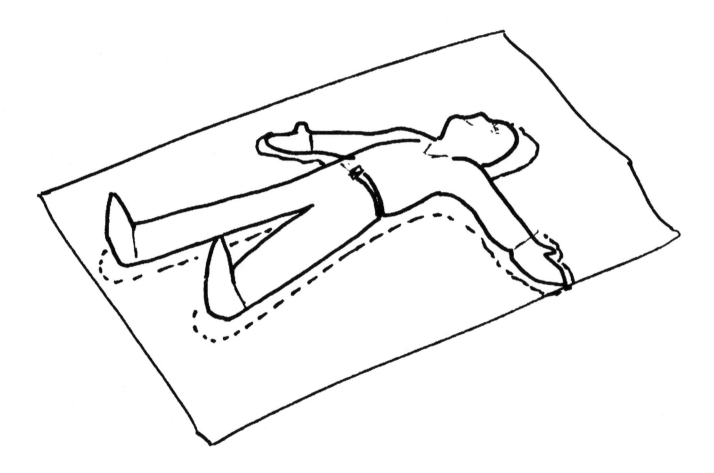

Praise God from Whom All Blessings Flow

Background Information

Composer: Thomas Ken (1637–1711)
Year of Publication: 1695
Tune: "Old Hundredth" by Louis Bourgeois (1510–1561)
Scripture References: Psalm 86:12; 2 Corinthians 13:14

Theme

Joy and praise bursts forth from those who recognize our triune God as Father, Son, and Holy Ghost.

Teaching Tool

rhythm instrument—tambourine

Suggestions for Dialogue and Discussion

Hello, Hello, Hello! [Shake sample tambourine.] Welcome, Welcome, Welcome! [Shake tambourine again.] How are you, How are you, How are you? [Shake tambourine again.] Do I seem to be repeating myself? Yes, I said everything three times, didn't I? That's because three is a special number that we want to think about today. Notice there are three streamers on my tambourine. [Point to streamers.] Each one is going to teach us something about a song sung by Christians probably more often than any other. We sing it in our church every week [or modify appropriately]. The song really has three names. [Point to lettering on tambourine.] It's earliest name was "Old Hundredth" because the tune was first used to sing Psalm 100. Another name you might recognize is *Doxology*, which is a Greek word meaning "offering praise to God." Maybe you know it best simply by the first line often used as its title, "Praise God from Whom All Blessings Flow." [Point out each name appropriately.] These three names all really mean the same song.

The song can first be found in the *Geneva Psalter* which was a book of tunes to which Christians could sing the Psalms from the Bible. The *Geneva Psalter* was first published over four hundred years ago! Scholars believe the "Old Hundredth" tune was probably written by a Frenchman named Louis Bourgeois. [Point to respective names on the first streamer.] But the person who wrote the words that we sing today was an outspoken Anglican bishop who was trying to teach his young scholars at Winchester College to say their prayers. His name was Thomas Ken. [Point to Ken's name.]

Thomas Ken wrote three hymns for his students to sing as part of their personal devotions: prayers for morning, for evening, and for midnight. [Indicate middle streamer's words.] At the end of each of those prayer-songs, was the "Doxology," words of praise to God [point to third streamer], as Father, Son, and Holy Spirit.

What Thomas Ken began as a way to teach just a school full of students to remember to praise God and seek God's help for life has now become probably one of the most frequently used hymns about God that Christians sing. Each week in churches everywhere voices are raised in praise of God. Now we can use our tambourines as we sing the "Doxology" and celebrate our God who is one God in three persons: Father, Son, and Holy Spirit. [Raise and shake tambourine after each name of God.]

Materials

- paper plates or aluminum pie pans; two per tambourine
- pebbles
- staples and stapler or tape
- crepe paper or ribbon
- markers
- scissors

Method

Create a rhythm instrument tambourine from sturdy paper plates or aluminum pie pans. Begin stapling or taping two plates or pans together. Before completely closing the tambourine, fill it with pebbles. Secure the two pieces together. Write *"Old Hundreth," "Doxology,"* and *"Praise God from Whom All Blessings Flow"* on one or both sides of the plates.

Cut three 12" to 18" streamers from crepe paper or wide ribbon. On the first strip write: *Geneva Psalter, Louis Bourgeois,* and *Thomas Ken.* On the second strip write: *Morning, Evening,* and *Midnight.* On the third strip write: *Father, Son,* and *Holy Spirit.* Staple the three strips to the bottom of the tambourine.

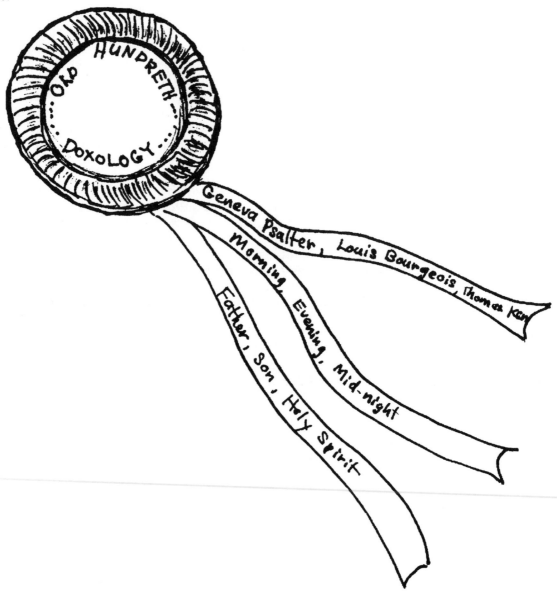

Rejoice, Ye Pure in Heart

Background Information

Composer:	Edward Hayes Plumptre (1821–1891)
Year of Publication:	1868
Tune:	"Marion" by Arthur Henry Messiter (1834–1916)
Scripture References:	Psalm 20:5; Philippians 4:4

Theme

Those who know God proclaim their love in praise and thanksgiving.

Teaching Tool

pennant banner and standard

Suggestions for Dialogue and Discussion

Have you ever been to a baseball game? [Allow sharing of responses.] Did you see anything that looked a little like this? [Hold up pennant banner.] I bet you saw lots of pennants. Maybe you even have a pennant or two hanging on your walls at home. What are pennants for? [Someone should be able to suggest "for cheering."] Yes! We cheer our favorite teams with pennants and let other people know whose side we're on. Well, this pennant doesn't have a team name on it. What does this say? [Let someone read the word *Rejoice.*]

Rejoice means to be glad and celebrate. Why would we rejoice in the church? [Many possibilities may be suggested. That's good!] We have lots of reasons to celebrate. That is why we gather on Sunday mornings—to celebrate God's presence with us. It's always more fun to celebrate with a crowd.

The hymn story we share today comes from a big celebration that was once planned at Peterborough Cathedral in England. Edward Plumptre was an Anglican minister and scholar who also liked to write poetry. Every year at Peterborough Cathedral they held a choir festival when lots of people from surrounding towns would gather to celebrate and sing together. As the service began, the combined choir would proceed into the cathedral singing. There were so many members in the festival choir that Edward had to write eleven stanzas to "Rejoice, Ye Pure in Heart" in order to get everyone in. I bet they carried in banners to proclaim whose side they were on as they all marched down the aisle. That would have been something to see, wouldn't it?

Banners have been important to people for a long time. They are declarations that something or someone important is arriving. In wartime, banners were often attached to a standard or spear that could be carried into battle and then planted by the victors when the battle was won.

In many ways, it would be a good idea if we Christians carried banners with us all the time. The cross on the standard could remind us of the King we serve. The word *rejoice* could remind us that every day God gives us is a blessing to celebrate. And we could let other people know whose side we're on! Edward Plumptre's message could become a part of our everyday lives: "Rejoice, give thanks, and sing!"

Materials

- screen molding (2 1/2 feet per standard)
- small saw, utility knife, or tin snips
- sand paper
- wood glue
- felt, paper, or suitable banner material
- scissors
- markers (optional)
- letter patterns
- fabric glue
- paint
- paint brush

Method

For each standard, cut one 6" and one 2' strip of screen molding. Sand lightly any rough edges. Paint the wood pieces, if desired. Glue the 6" cross piece about 3" from the top of the standard. Allow to dry. Attach a 16" to 18" pennant banner cut from felt or other suitable materials about 3" below the cross piece. Add letters for *REJOICE* with markers, or cut each letter from felt or paper and glue onto pennant.

Rock of Ages

Background Information

Composer:	Augustus M. Toplady (1740–1778)
Year of Publication:	1776
Tune:	"Toplady" by Thomas Hastings (1784–1872)
Scripture Reference:	1 Corinthians 10:4

Theme

Faith in the saving power of Jesus, our Rock, provides shelter, safety, and strength for life.

Teaching Tool

"rock" concentration game

Suggestions for Dialogue and Discussion

[Hold up the first rock on which is written the word *Toplady*. Encourage first "challenger" to choose a rock and try to make a match; keep taking turns among players until a match is found. Relate the information as the match is sought.] This rock says *Toplady*. That is a funny name. Can you find the matching rock? Augustus Toplady lived in England over two hundred years ago and wrote a famous hymn that we still sing today. The title has the word *rock* in it. Does anyone know? [Allow guesses; then inform if necessary that it is "Rock of Ages." Reward verbally the person who located the matching rock.] Now that we know that Toplady is the name of the composer of the hymn "Rock of Ages," let's see what other matches we can make.

[Hold up the rock that says *salvation*.] When Augustus Toplady was sixteen years old and living in Ireland, he went to a small church service that was held in a barn. As he listened to the simple message of Jesus' power to save, he was so moved that he gave his life to God's service and eventually became an Anglican minister, stirring the hearts of others to accept Christ's saving love.

[Hold up the rock that says *theology*.] This is a big word that means "what we believe about God." After Augustus Toplady became a minister, he argued theology with a man named John Wesley. Augustus wanted to prove his point that people always remained sinners and were saved only by the power of God. So he wrote a poem in 1776 about his beliefs.

[Hold up the rock that says *Hastings*.] Thomas Hastings was the one who set Toplady's poem to music. Thomas Hastings didn't have much formal music education, and he suffered problems with his eyes because he was born an *albino*, a person who has no color or pigment in his skin. But despite his problems, he became one of the most influential persons in shaping church music in the United States, writing over one thousand hymn tunes. Among them was the tune he named "Toplady" for the hymn "Rock of Ages."

[Hold up the last rock that says *Jesus*.] It will be easy to match the last of our rocks, won't it? [Some may express that the last two do not match.] Well, although my rock says *Jesus* and your rock says *Rock* that is still a match. Because, you see, the "Rock of Ages" is Jesus, the one who gives us safety, shelter, and strength for life. Jesus can be the foundation for our lives, just like He was for our hymn writers. Even though Augustus Toplady died at an early age from overwork and tuberculosis, the hymn he wrote endures today. And our faith can endure when it is placed in Jesus, the Rock of Ages.

Materials
- rocks (10 per game)
- permanent markers

Method

Prepare ten pieces for a game of Concentration by writing each of the following words on the number of rocks indicated in parenthesis: *Toplady* (2); *Salvation* (2); *Theology* (2); *Hastings* (2); *Jesus* (1); *Rock* (1).

Separate the rocks into two piles. Retain five rocks labeled *Toplady, Salvation, Theology, Hastings,* and *Jesus,* to use during the storytelling. Place the other five rocks within easy reach of the listeners. Begin the hymn story by inviting the group to play a game of Concentration. Explain that each rock contains a word associated with the song they will be singing and studying. When the leader displays one rock, the learners will attempt to locate the duplicate word by overturning rocks, one at a time, until a match is made.

At the conclusion of the message, or during another teaching time, provide ten rocks for each participant and invite the learners to make Concentration games to use in retelling the hymn story.

Savior, Like a Shepherd Lead Us

Background Information

Composer: Attributed to Dorothy Ann Thrupp (1779–1847)
Year of Publication: 1836
Tune: "Bradbury" by William Batchelder Bradbury (1816–1868)
Scripture References: Psalm 23; John 10:11

Theme

We are known to God because God made us; we are precious to God because Jesus bought us.

Teaching Tool

clothespin sheep and shepherd's staff

Suggestions for Dialogue and Discussion

[Hold up a sample sheep.] While I talk with you about our hymn story today, I want you to make your own sheep, okay? [Distribute materials; have as much already prepared as time constraints require. Give any needed directions.] Many stories from the Bible and many hymns of faith are about sheep. Did you ever realize that? One of the most famous hymns about Jesus the Good Shepherd is "Savior, Like a Shepherd Lead Us." One interesting point about this hymn is that no one knows for sure exactly who wrote the words. Many people believe that the author was a woman by the name of Dorothy Ann Thrupp, the daughter of an Anglican minister, who is known to have written many hymns for children. She lived in the early 1800s in England. And although she wrote many poems, she seldom signed her name to any of her works. If she did, she often used a *pseudonym*, a made-up name that authors call a "pen name." Do you think that's strange? Do you always put your names on what you create? Even if Dorothy had signed her name, back then when hymns were published in collections of poetry, the authors' names were often left out. So we can't be sure exactly who wrote "Savior, Like a Shepherd Lead Us," but Dorothy Thrupp seems a very likely choice.

How are your sheep coming along? Almost finished? Well, while you work I can also tell you a little about the man who wrote the music for this famous hymn. His name was William Bradbury. He was a very famous church musician who wrote many popular hymn tunes in his day. Maybe you have heard "Just As I Am," or "Sweet Hour of Prayer." Those are just two songs that William Bradbury wrote. He wrote an entire book of hymns to be used in Sunday school because he believed "good singing" was an important part of a successful program. It took both our anonymous poet and Mr. Bradbury to create this beautiful hymn, didn't it?

Well, I'd like to see how your sheep are coming along. Let's stand them up so that we can take a look. Even if you aren't quite finished, put the clothespin legs on and stand them up in a row. Look at all the sheep! You did such a nice job! What would happen if I moved the sheep all around and put them in different places? [Move them around, mixing them up.] Can you still tell which one is your sheep? [Have one child find his or her own, or if not too disruptive, allow each child to claim his or her own.]

That's amazing, isn't it? How can you tell your own sheep? [Allow responses. Most will say "because I made it."] When you make something yourself, you can recognize it, can't you? If Dorothy Thrupp were here, she could tell us if these words were hers. With human beings, there are no "anonymous" creations. You are created by God. God knows each one of you, just like you know your sheep.

But there is even more to the story. Jesus is our Good Shepherd. He leads us in life, just like a shepherd guides sheep with his staff. [Hook the sample crook around the sample sheep.] You can make a staff for your sheep, too. [Hand out pipe cleaners.] Even more important than leading us, Jesus laid down His life for us, paid the price for our sin. Our hymn says He "bought us."

Just like it took both Dorothy Thrupp and William Bradbury to give us this hymn, it takes both God the Creator and Jesus the Savior to give us an understanding of God's love.

Materials
- sheep pattern
- posterboard
- scissors
- clip clothespins (may be prepainted black)
- markers
- pipe cleaners

Method
Make a sample clothespin sheep. Trace the sheep pattern onto posterboard and cut out the shape. With a black marker, draw a face and outline the body of the sheep. Write the words *"Savior, Like a Shepherd Lead Us"* on the body of the sheep. If desired, spray paint the clothespins black. When the paint is dry, attach clothespins to the bottom of the sheep as legs. Bend one pipecleaner to form a shepherd's staff.

Sweet Hour of Prayer

Background Information

Composer:	Attributed to William W. Walford (1772–1850)
Year of Publication:	1845
Tune:	"Sweet Hour" by William B. Bradbury (1816–1868)
Scripture Reference:	Psalm 27:14; Philippians 4:6

Theme

At all times, Christians are called to prayer, giving concerns to God and receiving peace and power.

Teaching Tool

hourglass

Suggestions for Dialogue and Discussion

How much time have you spent lately breathing? [Invite responses.] Probably you will tell me you are constantly breathing, right? That's because oxygen is necessary for us to live. Well, as Christians we believe our souls have a need for prayer just as our lungs have a need for air. Have you ever spent an hour praying? [If some say "yes," encourage with "that's great!"] Studies show that the average Christian spends five minutes or less in prayer every day. Yet those same Christians probably have enthusiastically sung the hymn "Sweet Hour of Prayer." [Hold up hourglass to show title.] That song teaches us that we can tell God everything that we need or want and can escape evil by talking to God about our innermost feelings. "Sweet Hour of Prayer" tells us that prayer is trusting God, simply waiting in God's presence or "seeking God's face" until we catch a glimpse of heaven.

The problem is that we tend to quit too soon or to talk too much. This hour glass can help us learn to be better "pray-ers" by measuring time for us, and its two sides can remind us to spend time listening as well as speaking. [Show words on other side.]

As we watch the sand sift down, we can learn that there are also two stories to how "Sweet Hour of Prayer" was written. The first story was told by Thomas Salmon about a sight-impaired friend named William Walford who was a Congregational minister in England. Salmon said he wrote down the words as his friend dictated a poem he had composed but could not see to record. Thomas Salmon offered the words along with his story of how he came to acquire the poem to the *New York Observer* who published both Salmon's account and "Sweet Hour of Prayer."

On the other hand, William J. Reynolds, a modern author who researched this hymn story, could not verify Salmon's story. The William Walford he found in historical records was also a Congregational minister, but he lived in a different town, was sighted, and had published a book about prayer. This story just gets more and more complicated, doesn't it? Sometimes we feel like our lives are like that—full of contradictions and uncertainty. But regardless of who wrote "Sweet Hour of Prayer," the words are simple and true. And when sung to the tune William Bradbury wrote especially for these verses, we can be reminded to let go and trust God with all our cares and worries—sort of like exhaling problems and inhaling God's Spirit.

Now we're ready to practice increasing the amount of time we spend in prayer. We can use the hourglass to help us learn to wait in God's presence, both speaking and listening. And we can sing "Sweet Hour of Prayer" to remind us how important it is for Christians to pray—just like it's important to breathe!

Materials

- plastic bottles with flat bottoms (one or two liter pop bottles); two per hourglass
- cork; one per hourglass
- drill
- sand
- permanent markers
- electrical or duct tape

Method

Construct an hourglass from two bottles of the same size. Begin by washing and de-labeling the bottles. Be sure they are free of moisture before continuing the project. Fill one bottle with sand.

Find a cork that will fit into the neck of the bottle. Drill a hole through the center of the cork lengthwise. The size of the hole will determine the speed at which the sand flows from side to side. Join the two bottles with the single cork. Experiment with coarse and fine sand. When the sand empties from one bottle to the other in the desired length of time, secure the hourglass by taping the two necks together with electrical or duct tape.

Decorate the bottles with words and symbols related to the hymn "Sweet Hour of Prayer." On the top bottle write the following words, vertically, on the four sides:

Side One: *"Sweet Hour*
Side Two: *William Walford (Sight-impaired)*
Side Three: *Speaking*
Side Four: *Rev. Thomas Salmon*
Write the following words, vertically, on the second bottle:
Side One: *of Prayer"*
Side Two: *William Walford (Sighted)*
Side Three: *Listening*
Side Four: *William Reynolds*

Take My Life and Let It Be

Background Information

Composer:	Frances Ridley Havergal (1836–1879)
Year of Publication:	1874
Tune:	"Hendon" by Henri Alexander Cesar Malan (1787–1864)
Scripture References:	Matthew 22:37; Romans 12:1

Theme

Those who would be truly happy give everything to God.

Teaching Tool

felt story box

Suggestions for Dialogue and Discussion

[Hold up sample of box.] What kinds of things would you guess would be kept in a special box like this? [Children might guess watches and jewelry, or money.] I think those are good guesses. Those things are treasures we might expect to find in special keepsake boxes. But this box is to remind us of a special woman named Frances Havergal who lived a long time ago in England. [Show the name printed there.]

Frances Havergal was a woman who possessed many great abilities. She had a beautiful voice and great musical talent. She could have been rich and famous. But Frances knew she possessed even greater treasures than her musical gifts or money. She was a woman who measured her wealth by God's standards. One of the treasures she knew she possessed was simply the gift of life. [Place the shape of the torso on the felt-covered lid.] Where does the gift of life come from? [Someone will probably suggest "from God."] Yes, life is a gift of God.

Another gift Frances treasured was her hands. [Place the hands on the figure.] She was a kind and loving person who often prayed for people. Her hands were probably often folded in prayer. As well, she treasured another of God's gifts—feet. [Place the feet on the figure.] Now, that may seem silly to you, but Frances Havergal suffered as an invalid much of her life and was confined to a wheelchair. She probably treasured the gift of being able to walk more than those of us who take it for granted.

Besides her hands and feet, Miss Havergal knew the importance of the treasure of voice and lips. [Place mouth on figure.] Our voices give sound and our lips shape the words. And what we say can be either a blessing or a curse. If we treasure the gifts of speech and singing as gifts of God, we will want to use those abilities to bless everyone who hears us.

The next treasures may seem more like real treasures to you. But those who cannot use their hands or feet or those who cannot speak or sing would probably disagree with you. [Place silver and gold, one in each hand of figure.] Often the only treasures we think of are our silver and gold—our money. And they are real treasures. But Frances Havergal discovered that greater happiness comes from sharing one's wealth than from holding on to it. When she learned that the missionary society needed funds, she joyously packed up almost all of her jewelry from her jewelry box—over fifty pieces of valuable gold and silver—and sent them to the missionary society to use to get money for their work for God.

But probably the greatest gifts that Frances Havergal shared with people were her acts of love and the sharing of herself. [Place heart shape on figure.] When she was nearing the end of her life, she once visited with people who did not yet fully know Jesus. By her prayers, her love, and her selfless caring, all ten members of the family came to understand what it means to love and serve Christ. Frances was so happy for them to find God, that she stayed up that night and wrote twelve *couplets*, or rhyming lines, which we now sing as a hymn called "Take My Life."

What our hymn teaches is that we will only find true happiness in life by giving to God all the treasures we possess—our lives, our hands and feet, our voices and lips, our silver and gold, our love, our whole selves. Then our treasure will be even greater, because, like Frances Havergal, we will be filled with joy. And joy is the one treasure everyone is trying to find. Frances knew the secret. And now you do, too!

Materials

- cigar box with flip-top lid
- felt
- scissors
- glue
- permanent markers
- figure patterns

Method

As the illustration for the hymn "Take My Life and Let It Be" create a felt story box. Cover each side of the lid of a cigar box with a piece of felt. On the outside, with permanent marker, write the name of the hymn and information about the composer.

Using the illustrations provided, cut each piece of the figure from felt. Add details and decorations as desired. During the storytelling, place the shapes on the inside lid of the cigar box at the appropriate times.

This Is My Father's World

Background Information

Composer: Maltbie D. Babcock (1858–1901)
Year of Publication: 1901
Tune: "Terra Beata" by Franklin L. Sheppard (1852–1930)
Scripture References: Psalm 8; Psalm 121:1

Theme

All nature reminds those who look and listen to live with reverence for God's gifts of life and beauty.

Teaching Tool

family tree

Suggestions for Dialogue and Discussion

[Place sample Family Tree where participants can see wording and reach to add leaves.] Do any of you know what the word *genealogy* means? [Most will have no clue.] *Genealogy* is the study of family history, like, who your parents, grandparents, and great-grandparents were. All of us have a history, and so do all hymns. This is a "family tree" to help us discover the story behind a famous hymn called "This Is My Father's World." [Point to the words on the trunk.]

The first branch tells us the name of the man who penned the words we sing; his name was Maltbie D. Babcock. [Point out branch.] Here are some leaves that can add to our understanding of who Rev. Babcock was. [If possible, allow listeners to add the leaves as each is discussed.] That was your first hint—Rev. Babcock served as a minister in the Presbyterian church. [Attach leaf.] Often we think of ministers as being more interested in books and words, but Rev. Babcock was also a talented athlete who excelled in swimming and baseball. [Attach leaf.] He also had musical gifts and could play the organ, piano, and violin. [Attach leaf.] Obviously, he was also a poet because he left us these beautiful words to "This Is My Father's World," written just one year before he died at the early age of forty-three. [Add leaf.] Those who knew him best remembered his favorite hobby—walking in nature—and the words he always said just before he left: "I am going out to see my Father's world." In the original poem, there were sixteen verses, and each of them started with "This is my Father's world." [Attach leaf.]

Of course, on a family tree, we are never alone, there are always others whose lives influence and affect ours. It was Rev. Babcock's wife who saw to it that his poem was published after his death, and the last verse of the hymn we sing was written by his daughter, Mary Babcock Crawford. [Add leaves to branches.]

On a family tree we only add the names of those to whom we are related, but this family tree represents God's "family," so we can add others who also belong to God. Rev. Babcock's inspiring poem was set to music by a talented member of God's family and a warm, personal friend of the poet, Franklin L. Sheppard. His music, taken from an old English folk tune, was named *Terra Beata*, which is Latin for "blessed earth." [Add leaf.]

This next branch is for us—for you and me—because as God's children we belong to the family. The song reminds us that those who love God respond by looking at nature, listening to nature, and praising God for the beauty of our Earth. When we see the majesty of creation all around us and realize that God is the power behind all of nature that we see and hear, then we must realize that God is in control and we can trust God, like a small child trusts a loving father. [Add leaves.]

Like all living trees, God's family tree keeps growing. There are many, many branches and many, many leaves. Maybe today you will want to take a walk to see some real trees and will tell your earthly family, like Rev. Babcock often did, "I am off to see my Father's world."

Materials

- patterns for tree and leaf
- duplicating equipment
- construction paper
- scissors
- markers
- glue

Method

Duplicate a copy of the tree and the leaf for each participant. Prepare a sample "family tree" to use while telling the hymn story. Glue the tree to a sheet of construction paper. Cut eleven leaves from various colors of construction paper. Write the following words on the leaves:

For "Maltbie D. Babcock" branch:
Served as minister
Excelled in swimming and baseball
Played musical instruments
Wrote poetry
Walked in nature
For "Mrs. Babcock" branch:
Published poem
For "Mary Babcock Crawford" branch:
Wrote last verse
For "Franklin L. Sheppard" branch:
Composed music
For "God's Children" branch:
Look and listen for beauty
Praise God
Trust God

Attach the leaves to the branches in advance or during the children's message.

Illustration

tree with five branches

Tree trunk has words *"This Is My Father's World"* written on its branches, from left to right, reading:
- *Maltbie B. Babcock*
- *Mrs. Babcock*
- *Mary Babcock Crawford*
- *Franklin L. Sheppard*
- *God's Children*

leaf pattern

What a Friend We Have in Jesus

Background Information

Composer:	Joseph Medlicott Scriven (1819–1886)
Year of Publication:	c. 1869
Tune:	"Erie" by Charles Crozat Converse (1832–1918)
Scripture References:	Luke 18:1; Philippians 4:6

Theme

No matter what difficulties life brings, through prayer we find the help of our dearest friend, Jesus, and find the strength to share His love with others.

Teaching Tool

friendship heart

Suggestions for Dialogue and Discussion

[Hold up the half of the friendship necklace containing the name of Joseph Scriven.] Have you ever seen a friendship necklace? Sometimes when we have a very special person in our lives, we let him or her know how much we care by sharing matching necklaces. I would wear one half and my special friend would wear the other half. I made this one to help us remember the hymn story for today. This man is the poet who wrote the words to the hymn "What a Friend We Have in Jesus." His name is Joseph Scriven. He was born into a well-to-do family in Ireland, so he received an excellent education. He was going to marry the girl he loved, become a minister, and settle down to a happy and contented life. But guess what . . . his heart was broken when, on the night before they were to be married, his fiancée accidentally drowned. Joseph was unable to stay in Ireland because he was so unhappy; so he left for Canada and ended up in a city called Port Hope.

In Canada, Joseph Scriven decided that he knew how he wanted to spend the rest of his life—by being a friend to those in need. [Turn over the heart to show the word *Friend.* Hold up the second half of the heart that says *Poor and Needy* and *Mother.*] Joseph became known as the "Good Samaritan of Port Hope." Although he taught and ministered, he did most of his work without receiving any money. He took care of those people who had no one to befriend them and no way to repay him. In time, he even found another woman he loved and planned to marry. But tragically, after a brief illness, she, too, died before they could be married.

All of the difficulties in Joseph's life taught him that there was one way to cope with pain and loss. That was to talk with the very best friend a person can have. Can you guess who that friend might be? Right! That friend is Jesus. When his mother was struggling with a difficult situation far away from him in Ireland, Joseph wrote to her and sent a poem he had composed. He never intended anyone else but her to read it. He said that the Lord and he had written the words together. The words of that poem became the hymn text for one of the all-time favorite hymns anywhere. [Turn over the second half of the heart to reveal *in Jesus.*] Can you read the title? [Let children read "What a Friend We Have in Jesus."]

Interestingly, we wouldn't even know today that Joseph Scriven wrote this hymn, except that when he was sick a friend came to visit him and found the poem scribbled on some notepaper. Joseph explained that he had written the words to comfort his mother.

Despite all the tragedy and unhappiness in his life, Joseph discovered the source of healing for a broken heart. We have to get in touch with our dearest friend of all—Jesus. [Place the two halves of the heart together and thread them onto the ribbon or cord.] And then, we can share Jesus' love with others.

Materials

- heart pattern
- construction paper
- scissors
- markers
- ribbon or cord
- paper punch

Method

To make an illustration for the hymn "What a Friend We Have in Jesus," trace the heart pattern onto construction paper and cut out the two pieces. Punch a hole at the top of each half. Write the following words on the shapes:

Left Side Front: *Joseph Scriven*
Left Side Back: *"What a Friend We Have*
Right Side Front: *Poor and Needy; Mother*
Right Side Back: *in Jesus"*

Craft Projects

Resources

Elkins, Stephen. *This Is My Story*. Nashville: Stephen Elkins Music, 1988.

Emurian, Ernest K. *Stories of Christmas Carols*. Grand Rapids: Baker, 1958.

Idle, Christopher, compiler. *Christmas Carols and Their Stories*. Oxford: Lion, 1988.

_____ . *Famous Hymns and Their Stories*. Oxford: Lion, 1987.

_____ . *Lion Book of Famous Hymns, The*. Oxford: Lion, 1980.

_____ . *Songs of Faith*. Tring: Oxford, 1986.

Konkel, Wilbur. *Living Hymn Stories*. Minneapolis: Bethany House, 1982.

Loewen, Alice, Harold Moyer, and Mary Oyer. *Exploring the Mennonite Hymnal: Handbook*. Newton, KS: Faith and Life Press and Scottdale, PA: Mennonite Publishing House, 1983.

Lovelace, Austin C. *Hymn Notes for Church Bulletins*. Chicago: GIA, 1987.

Nelson, Ruth Youngdahl. *God's Song in My Heart*. Philadelphia: Fortress Press, 1957.

Osbeck, Kenneth W. *Amazing Grace: 366 Inspiring Hymn Stories for Daily Devotions*. Grand Rapids: Kregel Publications, 1990.

_____ . *52 Hymn Stories Dramatized*. Grand Rapids: Kregel, 1992.

_____ . *101 Hymn Stories*. Grand Rapids: Kregel, 1982.

_____ . *101 More Hymn Stories*. Grand Rapids: Kregel, 1985.

Rizk, Helen Salem. *Stories of the Christian Hymns*. Nashville: Abingdon, 1989.

Terry, Lindsay L. *Good Morning, Lord. Family Devotionals From Famous Hymns*. Grand Rapids: Baker, 1974.

Hymn Devotions for All Seasons. Nashville: Abingdon, 1989.

About the Authors

Phyllis Vos Wezeman

Phyllis Vos Wezeman is Executive Director of the Parish Resource Center of Michiana, Inc. Phyllis has served as Adjunct Faculty at Indiana University South Bend, from which she holds an M.S. in Education; a consultant or board member to numerous local and national organizations; and has led a six-week youth exchange program to Russia and the Ukraine.

Author or coauthor of over 250 books and articles on creative approaches to education, she has written *Peacemaking Creatively Through the Arts* (Prescott, AZ: Educational Ministries, Inc., 1990) and *Joy to the World* (Notre Dame, IN: Ave Maria Press, 1992). Phyllis, the 1992 recipient of the Aggiornamento Award presented by the Catholic Library Association for fostering a spirit of renewal and interfaith outreach, is the first Protestant to receive this honor.

Anna L. Liechty

Anna L. Liechty is a public school teacher and Christian educator who teaches English in Plymouth, Indiana. Ann holds an M.S. in Education from Indiana University South Bend and has taught youth and adults from middle school to undergraduate level. As well, her background and experience in writing and drama have led to many opportunities for dramatizations of Biblical characters and stories within religious education and worship settings.

Phyllis and Ann

have coauthored *Festival of Faith: A Vacation Church School Curriculum Celebrating the Gifts of God* (Prescott, AZ: Educational Ministries, Inc., 1993), *Instruments of Inspiration: An Advent and Christmas Worship Resource* (Mishawaka, IN: Active Learning Associates, Inc., 1993), and *Lessons for Lent: Learning About Jesus Through His Names* (Prescott, AZ: Educational Ministries, Inc., 1994).

Phyllis serves as President and Ann as Vice President of Active Learning Associates, Inc., a company dedicated to providing creative choices for experiential learning within congregation and community.